FOREWORD BY **CYRUS MAD-BONDO**

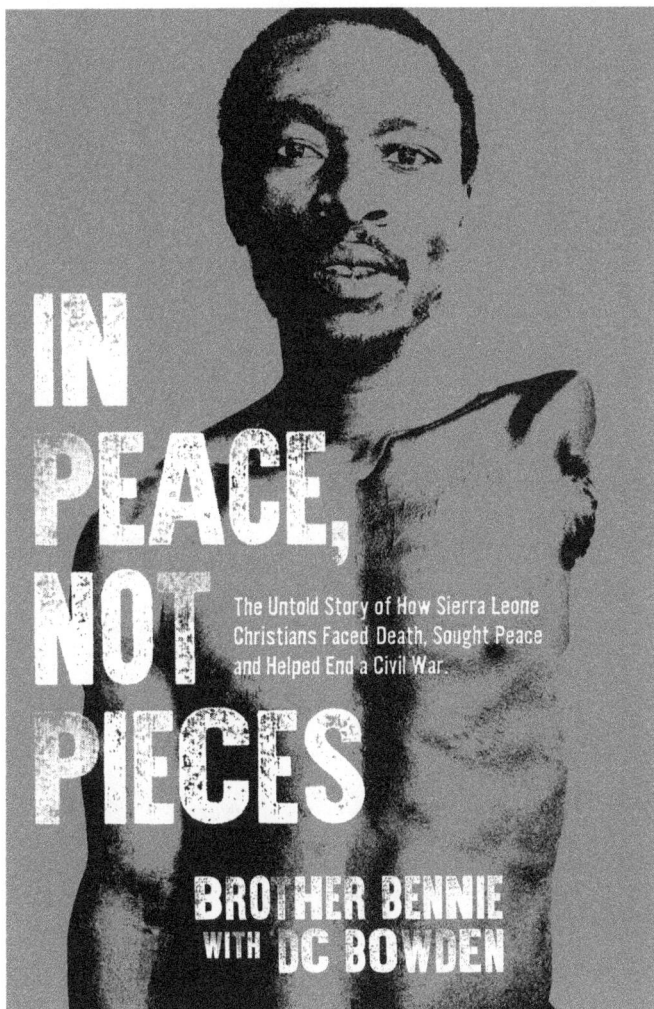

IN PEACE, NOT PIECES

The Untold Story of How Sierra Leone
Christians Faced Death, Sought Peace
and Helped End a Civil War.

BROTHER BENNIE
WITH **DC BOWDEN**

Alpha Ministries
Your Global Partner in the Gospel since 1965

Lynchburg, Virginia

IN PEACE, NOT PIECES

The Untold Story of How Sierra Leone Christians Faced Death, Sought Peace and Helped End a Civil War

Cover & Interior design: Roark Creative, www.RoarkCreative.com

Heartfelt thanks to David & Sandy Stratton for final edits.

A publication of Alpha Ministries Inc.,

ISBN number: **978-0-578-23631-5**

For information about our mission, write to:

Alpha Ministries
P.O. Box 4563
Lynchburg, VA 24502-4563
434-929-2500
www.AlphaMinistries.com

DEDICATED TO THE PEOPLE OF SIERRA LEONE

Sierra Leone, a country in West Africa, has a special significance in the history of the transatlantic slave trade as the departure point for thousands of west African captives. The capital, Freetown, was founded as a home for repatriated former slaves in 1787.

Capital of the Republic of Sierra Leone: **Freetown**

Population: **7.4 million**

Languages: **English, Krio (Creole language derived from English) and range of African languages**

Major Religions: **Islam and Christianity**

"If a commission by an earthly king is considered an honor, how can a commission by a Heavenly King be considered a sacrifice?"

—DAVID LIVINGSTON

David Livingston was a Scottish medical missionary to Africa. Known for being a doctor, pioneer and explorer, Livingston is almost legendary because of his ventures. He passed on the legacy of valuing the lives of the African people, as well as standing firmly against the slavery he witnessed. He did not consider the ruggedness of his life and experiences to be a hard sacrifice for Christ, but rather a privilege.

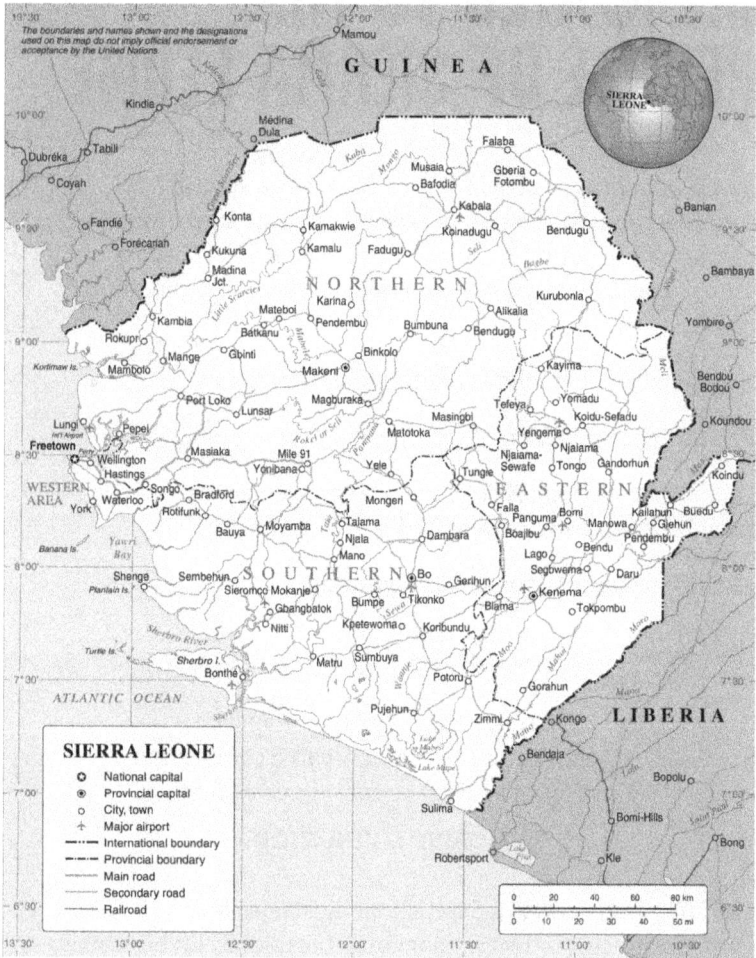

GUINEA

SIERRA LEONE

Mamou

Kindia
Médina Dula
Falaba
Musaia
Gberia Fotombu
Bafodia
Dubréka
Tabili
Coyah
Kabala
Konta
Fandié
Kamakwie
Koinadugu
Bendugu
Banian
Forécariah
Kukuna
Kamalu
Fadugu
Madina Jct.
NORTHERN
Bambaya
Karina
Kurubonla
Kambia
Matebol
Pendembu
Alikalia
Yombire
Batkanu
Bumbuna
Bendugu
Rokupr
Mange
Gbinti
Binkolo
Bendou Bodou
Kortimaw Is.
Mamboto
Makeni
Kayima
Port Loko
Lunsar
Magburaka
Teleya
Yomadu
Koundou
Masingbi
Koidu-Sefadu
Lungi
Int'l Airport
Pepel
Matotoka
Yengema
Njaiama
Freetown
Wellington
Masiaka
Mile 91
Yele
Njaiama-Sewafe
Tongo
Gandorhun
Hastings
Yonibana
Tungie
Koindu
WESTERN AREA
Songo
Bradford
Mongeri
Falla
EASTERN
York
Waterloo
Rotifunk
Panguma
Bomi
Manowa
Giehun
Buedu
Bauya
Moyamba
Talama
Dambara
Boajibu
Bendu
Pendembu
Njala
Lago
Kailahun
Mano
Segbwema
Daru
Shenga
Sembehun
SOUTHERN
Bo
Gerihun
Plantain Is.
Sieromco Mokanje
Bumpe
Tikonko
Kenema
Tokpombu
Banana Is.
Yawri Bay
Gbangbatok
Nitti
Kpetewoma
Koribundu
Blama
Turtle Is.
Sherbro River
Matru
Sumbuya
Sherbro I.
Bonthe
Potoru
Gorahun
ATLANTIC OCEAN
Pujehun
Zimmi
Kongo
LIBERIA
Bendaja
Bopolu
Sulima
Bomi-Hills
Bong
Robertsport
Kle

Rivers: Kaba, Mongo, Kaba, Seli, Bagbe, Little Scarcies, Great Scarcies, Rokel or Seli, Pampana, Sewa, Sherbro River, Moa, Mano

SIERRA LEONE

- ◉ National capital
- ⊛ Provincial capital
- ○ City, town
- ✛ Major airport
- ┅┅ International boundary
- ╌╌ Provincial boundary
- ── Main road
- ── Secondary road
- ── Railroad

0   20   40   60   80 km
0   10   20   30   40   50 mi

Sierra Leone

CONTENTS

Foreword   9

Introduction   13

Prayer   17

Chapter 1   Short Sleeve or Long Sleeve?   19

Chapter 2   Free at Last   27

Chapter 3   Rumors of War   39

Chapter 4   Unfortunately, I Met with Them   49

Chapter 5   Surviving the "Rescuers"   63

Chapter 6   I Don't Care   73

Chapter 7   The Road Less Taken   83

Chapter 8   Operation No Living Thing   93

Chapter 9   Bullets into Crosses   101

Chapter 10   The Butchers Become the Peacemakers   115

Glossary   123

Endnotes   124

FOREWORD

The book you are holding in your hands tells the raw truth about what countless people have suffered and overcome in Sierra Leone. Thousands were brutally killed during the 11 years of civil war. What would be the appropriate way of honoring their death? It is to make sure the preaching of the Gospel continues so that people are set free to love and respect one another.

Benny and Daniel painstakingly share story after story of people of all ages who have suffered or been brutally killed. As difficult as it was for me to read these stories, I could not help but thank God for the fact that they have been recorded to teach the surpassing value of a human life as well as teach the current and next generation of Africans to treasure peace because of the death of these thousands of Sierra Leoneans.

Countless Christian leaders have dared to live out the claims of the Gospel of Jesus Christ who say that he is the Prince of Peace. They have been willing to face the perpetrators and pray for their souls to be saved. Time and time again, these Christian leaders have preached the uncompromising truth of the gospel, as well as distributed Bibles, to the very rebels who killed innocent people in villages and towns.

I traveled to Sierra Leone last summer. It was a memorable trip for me because the people continue to work very hard to rebuild their country. It now makes sense to read what Benny and Daniel noted: "In 2011, Sierra Leone sent peacekeeping troops to Darfur. A newspaper headline read, '*The Butchers Become the Peacekeepers.*'" Is this really possible? The answer is a resounding yes. Only when one can examine—as well as juxtapose—this newspaper headline with the following recommendation from Matthew Parris, can one appreciate how profound these words are.

You see, Matthew Parris is a professed atheist who was actually born in Johannesburg, South Africa. He has crisscrossed the African continent and is quite familiar with the complexities of these intra-African conflicts. But he admits the valuable contribution of Christianity. "Now a confirmed atheist, I've become convinced of the enormous contribution that Christian evangelism makes in Africa: sharply distinct from the work of secular NGOs, government projects and international aid efforts. These alone will not do..."

It sounds counterintuitive and borderline offensive to entertain the thought that it is possible a butcher from Sierra Leone can become a peacekeeper in Darfur, Sudan. This reminds me of the story of the life of Saul who became Paul in the Bible. He was a murderer of Christians who became a messenger of the faith he was trying to destroy. And Sierra Leone is a country where people have been killed at the hands of their own countrymen!

The truth of those observations is one of the reasons why this book has been written. It is possible through faith in Jesus Christ for the vilest offender who believes, that a true transformation can result and impact society at large. When the vilest offender through faith in Jesus Christ truly believes, that true transformation can impact a society at large. I am originally from the Central African Republic. This country has seen countless killings, just like what Benny and Daniel have described in this book. Less than 3 years ago, Rwanda sent 1,500 soldiers as peacekeepers to my country where thousands have been killed at the hands of their own countrymen. In Rwanda, in 1994, in just 90 days, 1.1 million people were killed. The Rwandan Genocide was not from without but from within. The people of Rwanda have learned and chosen to forgive each other in order to live in peace. I have met personally with perpetrators of the genocide who have been reconciled to their victims in the village of Mbyo, Rwanda and they are living side by side in peace. Indeed, Benny and Daniel are correct to say that when the Prince of Peace sets up housekeeping in people's hearts, no matter what their country of origin, their conduct begins to reflect His Lordship.

The truth of the matter is, good has come out of the atrocities of the thousands of people killed in Sierra Leone. This book is a reminder to us that the Gospel does indeed transform lives and society, not just in Sierra Leone, but anywhere around the world.

May you wrestle with the reality of these atrocities and yet realize that each one of us can play a part as recommended by this book. Pray, give, go and support Sierra Leone for the glory of God.

CYRUS MAD-BONDO
Pastor of Mobilization, Global Outreach
McLean Bible Church, Tysons Campus

INTRODUCTION

You may remember hearing the term "blood diamond". Or maybe you watched *Blood Diamond*, the 2006 movie featuring Leonardo DiCaprio. He played a diamond smuggler caught in the middle of the Sierra Leone Civil War.

For many of us, that's all we know about Sierra Leone—something vague about diamonds, war, or child soldiers. I admit that before I traveled to Sierra Leone I didn't know as much as I should have. I was aware of many Christian efforts in Africa but I never heard anyone pray or plan to do anything for Sierra Leone.

Then I traveled to Sierra Leone. I spent time in Freetown, the capital city and traveled to some of the furthest rural areas. The people living in those areas shared their needs and showed me the scars of war on their bodies and their land. While I may have witnessed many heartbreaking things that made me weep, I also saw a vibrant and growing church in Sierra Leone. This church grew out of the ashes of the eleven-year Civil War and brokered the peace agreements that began the healing process for Sierra Leone and all of West Africa.

I read an article written by atheist BBC reporter Matthew Parris. It was formally published in The Times in December 2008 and later republished on the Richard Dawkins Foundation website. The title is striking: *As an Atheist, I Truly Believe Africa Needs God.*

He wrote, "Now a confirmed atheist, I've become convinced of the enormous contribution that Christian evangelism makes in Africa: sharply distinct from the work of secular NGOs, government projects and international aid efforts. These alone will not do. Education and training alone will not do. In Africa, Christianity changes people's hearts. It brings a spiritual transformation. The rebirth is real. The change is good."

Parris is by no means a defender of Christianity. But even he could not deny the true change only Christianity has brought and continues to bring to Africa. But he had to see it first. He had to witness it. We don't have much time to look these days. We fix our eyes downward on our phones, and even when we read headlines we're far removed from their reality. We must look up and into the eyes of the suffering.

When Jesus saw Mary and her friends weeping over the death of Lazarus, He was moved and wept too. He went. He saw and He wept. Let us follow his example and rightly weep over the things that make him weep. May we have a burden for those who are lost. May we have a heart like his! May our prayer be, "Let my heart be broken with the things that break the heart of God."

We cannot see without God's help so we must ask him to help us see. That is the reason Elisha prayed, "O Lord, open his eyes so he can see" before "the Lord opened the servant's eyes and he saw that the hill was full of horses and chariots of fire all around Elisha." (2 Kings 6:17) Paul also prays in Ephesians 1:18 "that the eyes of your heart may be enlightened so that you will know what the hope of His calling is."

My hope is that this book opens your eyes to the great need in Sierra Leone so that your heart may be burdened with the same burdens of our African brothers and sisters in Christ. Also, that you will rejoice with them in God bringing peace and breathing life into a country torn apart by war.

Africa

*"If you think you have come to the
mission field because you are a little better than others,
or as the cream of your church, or because of your medical
degree, or for the service you can render the African church,
or even for the souls you may see saved, you will fail. Remember,
the Lord has only one purpose ultimately for each one of us,
to make us more like Jesus. He is interested in your relationship
with Himself. Let Him take you and mold you as He will;
all the rest will take its rightful place."*

—HELEN ROSEVEARE

Helen Roseveare was also a doctor and missionary to Africa, specifically in the Congo. She trained nurses and ran a center where she treated leprosy and handled maternity issues. When civil war broke out in her region, Helen was one of several missionaries who were held captive by rebel forces. She was beaten, terrorized, and brutally raped. However, despite her unimaginable circumstances, Helen experienced deep relationship with Jesus. Amid heartbreaking suffering, she realized that Jesus understood every part of what she was going through. The Lord used this time in her life to mold her into an even more influential woman for Him.

Papa God,

Wi de kam bifo u wit kol at en noto wit wahala.

Salone, Preya

Lord,

We come before you in peace, not pieces.

— SIERRA LEONE PRAYER IN KRIO

1

SHORT SLEEVE OR LONG SLEEVE?

And a woman having an issue of blood for twelve years,
who had spent all her living on physicians, but could
not be healed by anyone...

LUKE 8:43

heku Conteh tried to look anywhere but straight ahead toward the front of the line. He tried to block out the agonized screams. But he could not. He heard the quick swish of a machete slicing through the air and then the dull thud as it hit the ground. Another scream. The line inched forward. Another slice. Another scream. He could run but it would only be worse. He would never make it deep enough into the Sierra Leone jungle in time and would be tortured or gunned down. All he could do was inch forward relentlessly. He looked down at his arms and hoped he would keep at least one. The blood from the amputees flowed off the riverside trail and down into the river, turning the water a deep reddish-brown. Sheku took another step forward.

The night before, Revolutionary United Front soldiers burned Sheku's entire village to the ground. The young women were raped, tortured in other ways and killed. The youngest and the oldest were the first to be executed since they were of no use to RUF forces. Those who were left alive had a choice. They could either serve the rebels as sex slaves, porters, soldiers or be killed on the spot. Sheku had sent his wife and two small children away the night before the invasion. Knowing he had to do whatever it took to see them again, he chose to live. Thirty-eight young men had been taken captive from his northern Sierra Leone village and forced to carry heavy supplies through the jungle. It could have been worse.

After marching for hours, the commander stopped the group along the riverbank. He randomly picked out fifteen of the thirty-eight prisoners and casually told his soldiers, many of them as young as fifteen years old, to kill them.

Sheku's friends and neighbors fell to their knees and begged for their lives. Others stood stoically, accepting their fate. There was no chance of escape. Their reality was standing before a child ready to pull the trigger of an AK-47.

A younger officer cautiously approached the commander and said, "Commander, these men…they did not resist."

Sheku and the other men exclaimed that yes, they had all indeed volunteered—under threat of death—to go with the rebels.

The commander looked down the row of men for a moment, considering their appeal.

"OK. Let them live. Only take one arm from each of them," The commander said casually.

Sheku was the last man in line that day. He looked down at his arms, wondering which one it would be. He waited for the dreaded question, "Short sleeve or long sleeve?" Did he want them to cut at his hand or his elbow? But the question never came. They grabbed his arm and swung. By the time it was his turn, the blade had grown dull. The process was not quick or painless.

When the final blow was rendered, Sheku fell backwards in

shock. The soldiers looked down and laughed. He finally managed to stand on his feet and fled into the woods with the other bleeding amputees, leaving the pieces of his arm behind on the banks of the river.

———————

I fly very frequently—typically lengthy international flights to India—in the economy section of the plane. But in 2004, I was flying from India to visit the country of Ghana for the first time and just as I was about to board, the agent informed me that I had been upgraded to business class.

The news made my day and provided an incredible experience flying into a new country!

I was all ready to enjoy the comfort and ample leg room of my new seating assignment.

Getting on a flight at early dawn is very tiring so such comfort is a rare privilege to be enjoyed. Such surprises usually set the stage for me to share with the person next to me about how God provides for and encourages me. Unfortunately, the person sitting next to me did not want to have any eye contact or conversation. He was busy getting settled and then the flight attendant started serving beverages, so he was occupied once more. He seemed very serious and his clothes suggested he was a distinguished African businessman or perhaps a United Nations representative from Africa.

Finally, before landing in Accra, Ghana, the crew was serving snacks and talking about landing procedures. They said those going to Freetown had to remain seated and keep their boarding passes for security check. Those getting off in Accra needed to show their boarding pass at the gate. I had a difficult time deciphering the announcements because of the static from the PA system and the announcer's thick accent. I asked the man seated next to me, "What are they saying about Freetown? Does this not go to Accra?" For the first time in hours, he turned to me with a smile and asked my destination.

I told him I was going to Accra and he explained the plane would land there to refuel before flying another two hours to Freetown, the capital city of Sierra Leone. He explained that Sierra Leone had been in civil war for years and airline businesses had just started flying there again but the only route was a stop for refueling in Ghana.

I tried to mentally place Sierra Leone on a map. I knew it was close to Ghana, somewhere in West Africa. Recognizing my "opening," I said, "This seat is what I like to call a F.O.G., a Favor of God." I began to tell him who I was, what I did and why I was on my way to Ghana. "In a nutshell," I explained, "soap, soup and salvation. If they are dirty, we clean them up. If they are hungry, we fill them up. And if they don't know God, we give them the Word."

The man looked at me and said, "Brother Bennie, you should come to Freetown." I confessed to him I didn't know too much about Sierra Leone. There was a pause and with a heaviness in his voice, he began to tell me about the bloody eleven-year civil war and the atrocities that men and women like Sheku experienced.

The hum of the circulating cabin air grew distant as he spoke. My mind became filled with terrible images of a country boiling over in unimaginable war and miserable poverty. He described a twisted wreck of mass-murdering war criminals, orphans, slaves and child soldiers all caught in a war waged by a myriad of nations, groups and confusing acronymic factions: RUF, SLA, EO, NPFL, CDF, ECOMOG and AFRC. Each was fighting for control over Sierra Leone's greatest resource, tiny little pieces of invaluable compressed earth known as diamonds.

It was 1991 when the Revolutionary United Front, or RUF, rose up against the Sierra Leone government and President Joseph Momoh. RUF was not a typical army, at least not in the way we think of an army. It was a ragtag mob of uneducated drug and alcohol addled teenagers who wielded a vicious array of weapons and destroyed anything in their path. They were led by Liberian and Libyan backed ruthless ex-military leaders. The founder of

RUF was Foday Saybana Sanko who was born in Sierra Leone and radicalized in his youth. After a first failed attempt to overthrow the government of Sierra Leone, he fled to Libya and aligned himself with Muammar al-Qaddafi. Later, he aligned himself with Charles Taylor, Liberian antigovernment guerrilla unit, the National Patriotic Front of Liberia. Now, Foday and his army were coming to topple Sierra Leone's government and take all the diamonds they wanted along the way.

Under the slogan of "No More Slaves, No More Masters. Power and Wealth to the People" Foday and his army terrorized their way through Sierra Leone, starting in the east and working westward to the coastal city of Freetown. No village was safe. The women were raped, tortured in depraved ways and slaughtered. The youngest children were killed. Children from about eight years of age and up were forced to shoot their parents and weaker siblings. The fittest children were taken prisoner, either to become child soldiers or to be forced to work in the diamond pits until they collapsed and died in the mud from exposure and exhaustion.

RUF's favorite method of torture was the amputation of limbs with a machete or axe. Sometimes it was one arm. Other times it was two. It all depended on the mood of the rebel in charge.

For eleven long years, the people of Sierra Leone endured one of the most terrifying and brutal civil wars in modern history. The country cried out to the entire world for help. As a former British colony, they pleaded with the western world for salvation and deliverance. But peace, while often within grasp, eluded Sierra Leone and her people for over a decade. The help the world did give Sierra Leone often brought only corruption and more destruction through bungled peace attempts and fundamental misunderstandings about the war itself.

All the while, the Christians in Sierra Leone cried out to God for salvation. They felt like the woman with the issue of blood told of in the Gospels. She had suffered for twelve long years until Jesus healed her. And the Christians of Sierra Leone suffered eleven bloody years crying out for the same healing.

Just as Jesus healed the woman and told her in Luke 8:48, "Go in peace and be freed from your suffering," he answered the cries of the church in Sierra Leone. Through national fasts, days of prayer and fearlessly meeting with the rebels in the bush, the Christian church succeeded in ending the war and bringing peace in ways no governmental agency or NGO ever did.

I could only shake my head as I imagined what this man sitting next to me had experienced; the friends and family he had lost, the suffering he had endured, and the poverty he saw every day. I sat in silence for a few moments and I asked him what he did for a living. He said with a slight smile, "Well, I am the mayor of Freetown."

He handed me his card and said, "Come. My people need your help."

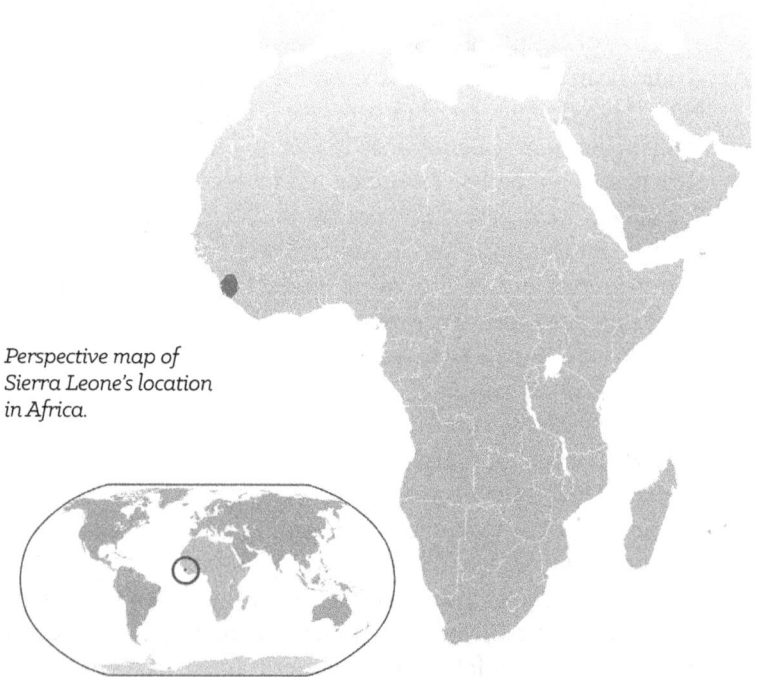

Perspective map of Sierra Leone's location in Africa.

Brother Bennie with Mr. Modetus Ahiable, former regional minister and High Commissioner to Benin in President Mills party, Ghana, West Africa.

Brother Bennie gifting a copy of his book Passage to the Unreached to former first lady Mrs. Ernestina Naadu Mills. She is the widow of President John Atta Mills, a legal scholar and President of Ghana, 2009-2012. President Mills went to be with the Lord on July 24, 2012.

2

FREE AT LAST

*Ye slaves of sin and hell, your liberty receive; and safe
in Jesus dwell, and blest in Jesus live. The year of jubilee
is come; return, ye ransomed sinners, home...*

BLOW YE THE TRUMPET, BLOW:
Hymn by Jonathan Edwards[1]

On March 11, 1792, a ship loaded with former slaves of the British Empire landed off the coast of Sierra Leone. As the sailors and freed slaves walked up the shore, they saw a massive cottonwood tree with large spreading branches in the distance that would give them shade from the afternoon heat. Under the tree, they held a worship service to God offering thanksgiving prayers and singing hymns. One of those songs was "Blow Ye the Trumpet, Blow." This new settlement was then dedicated to God and named Freetown. Ransomed slaves and sinners were finally home.

Those former slaves had won their freedom by fighting in the American Revolutionary War for the British. Some of them had been kidnapped not too many years earlier, all along the west coast of Africa. They had been taken captive, thrown into ships and sent throughout the western world.

It was slaves from the Sierra Leone Mende tribe who started the famous revolt aboard the ship, *La Amistad*. Eventually, the slaves aboard that ship were declared free by the United States Supreme Court and returned to Sierra Leone in 1842 with funds raised by the African-American Christian group, United Missionary Society.[2]

The notoriety of the *La Amistad* case fueled American missions to Sierra Leone resulting in churches, schools and vocational training.[3] Christianity spread through the efforts of western missionaries who toiled for God in the West African heat, burying their wives and children in the red dirt along the way. Missionaries like John Bowen, who put his hand to the plow of Sierra Leonean hearts and never looked back. Upon the death of his wife and baby in Freetown in 1858, Bowen wrote,

> *"Perhaps, delighting in her, I was getting to love the world too well; and if blessed with a boy, with my dear wife twining round my heart, I might have grown too fond of them, though I could not have been in one sense; yet I looked upon her perhaps too much as in the world, that is, as being my happiness here, and God has shewn me she was not of earth, but of heaven."*[4]

Former slaves were free men and those free men served God. These were the great spiritual riches upon which Freetown and modern Sierra Leone were founded. It seemed tailormade for a prosperous country with a people who cherished the principles of freedom.

The country those newly freed men came to possess was also rich in physical resources. Sitting on the Atlantic Ocean along the west coast of Africa and the deepest natural harbor in the world, Sierra Leone possesses everything you'd expect to see: white sandy beaches meeting dense mangrove swamps that slowly rise into wooded foothills upon which Freetown rises up along the horizon. Moving east, the hills level out into a grassland plateau which then rises sharply to lush, tropical and dense mountainous jungles. Eventually, it merges into the borders of Liberia and Guinea.

Portuguese explorer Pedro de Sintra saw those hills and mountains in 1462 and proclaimed it the land of the Lioness Mountains or Serra de Leoa in Portuguese. Some say he named it because of the shape of the mountains. Others claim it was the rolling thunder across the mountains which sounded like the roar of the African lion; the same thunder that still rumbles across the hills of Freetown during rainy season.

Freetown is where the sixteen ethnic tribes of Sierra Leone have melded together and now live side by side, the largest being the Temne from the north and the Mende from the south. There are also the descendants of the slaves, thought to number about 60,000 and are known as Creoles. They speak their own language called Krio, which is an interesting mix of English and indigenous West African languages. Unlike so many other African countries, however, there are virtually no ethnic or religious divisions in Sierra Leone. The Rwanda Genocide occurred in 1994 when the ethnic division between the Hutus and Tutsis boiled over. But the civil war in Sierra Leone had virtually no ethnic or religious component to it. People are loyal to their ethnic group but it has never been a cause for widespread violence. And while Sierra Leone is rife with African Traditional Religions (ATR) along with Christianity and Islam, it is considered one of the most tolerant countries in all of Africa. People intermarry among tribes and sometimes between religions.

Almost all the strife and divisions in Sierra Leone rose up not from ethnicities or religions, but from the soil. The soil of Sierra Leone holds untold wealth and riches in the form of rutile (a titanium ore), bauxite (an aluminum ore), gold and diamonds. In fact, 90 percent of all Sierra Leone exports are products from its vast mining industry. The country is consistently one of the top exporters of diamonds and producers of rutile.[5]

Diamonds are found in roughly a quarter of the country, covering 7,700 square miles. But the main production areas are in the districts of Bo, Kono and Kenema. Sierra Leone diamond exports regularly exceed USD$100 million annually. This brings more hope, wealth, poverty and war to Sierra Leone than any other resource. Diamonds have driven the greed of so many who have, in turn, laid waste to the country.[6]

The story of Sierra Leone's diamonds really began with De Beers Consolidated Mines Limited. Cecil Rhodes began diamond mining in Africa in the 1880s and quickly built an empire that now controls two-thirds of all diamonds in the world today, naming the entire African territory of Southern Rhodesia (now Zimbabwe) after himself. Rhodes formed the London Diamond Syndicate, which gave him leverage over all diamond supply and demand. The syndicate also allowed him to create an artificially controlled supply of diamonds which literally helped to define a fairly common stone as a rare and precious gem.

Through his company, Rhodes took total legal control of all of Sierra Leone's diamond mining in 1935. He partnered with Lebanese traders who quickly realized how much money could be made by smuggling diamonds out of the country. Mining was easy too. Illegal miners numbered in the tens of thousands. The Sierra Leone government took little action except to secure mining in Kono in the east and at the port in Freetown, leaving an easily accessible illegal trade route through Liberia. That pipeline of illegal diamonds would fuel an insatiable appetite for wealth among African warlords like Charles Taylor and Gaddafi which would, in turn, fund terrorism and wars for decades.

As a result, the illegal diamonds are known as Blood Diamonds or Conflict Diamonds, and it has been estimated that of all the diamonds in the world, 4 to 5 percent are blood diamonds. This tiny percentage has accounted for 3.7 million deaths and the displacement of 6 million people across Africa.[7]

The men, women and children prying these diamonds from the ground earn less than a single dollar a day. They have no training or safety equipment and severe injuries and deaths are common from landslides, mine collapses, poor sanitation and preventable diseases. In a single African province, Lunda Norte in Angola, it was discovered that 46 percent of the diamond miners were between the ages of 5 and 16.[8]

While in Freetown, I met a tall man with a deep voice named Alpha Marah. He knows fully well the price of diamonds. After fleeing a rebel attack and then surviving a botched joint SLA and Kamajor rescue operation on his village, Marah traveled to Tongo near the eastern border to work in a diamond mine. At that point in the conflict, the diamond mines were controlled by the rebels whose managerial style was even worse than the inhumane conditions normally experienced by miners.

One day Marah stood knee-deep in muddy water, bent over as he sifted the watery gravel through a mesh grate. A rebel guard ran over and accused the worker next to him of swallowing a diamond. Marah wasn't sure if the man actually swallowed the diamond and the guard wasn't either, but it didn't matter. The rebels were determined to try and retrieve the diamond if he had swallowed it. They dragged him to the shore and cut him open before digging inside his stomach while he was still alive. They did not find a diamond. Marah told me that was just a typical day and any attempt to steal a diamond resulted in a bullet to the head. Some workers would even lie to the guards about another worker for revenge, knowing the guards would have the person killed.

Marah saw many workers killed; his intense labor interrupted by the sharp crack of an AK-47 round exploding through the stifling jungle air. He didn't need to look up to know that another Sierra Leonean had become a victim of his country's greatest resource.

Those bright and beautiful diamonds, along with all the other resources of Sierra Leone, have been both a hope and a curse. That irony has been called the 'Resource Curse' or the 'Paradox of Plenty', a concept that tries to explain why many countries with abundant natural resources have always seemed to struggle with poverty, armed conflict and corruption.[9] Diamonds across Africa have been the primary tool for financing the very corruption and violence that have destroyed those countries from the inside. National leaders have grown insanely wealthy while entire infrastructures have collapsed and millions have suffered needlessly.

The diamonds of Sierra Leone funded RUF. Without them, the war could never have continued. They would not have been able to buy the weapons and ammo they needed. Those diamonds had to be taken through violent force and controlling the mines meant driving locals out through mass exiles.

Sierra Leone is now one of the poorest countries in the world. According to the UNDP Human Development Index, it ranks 184th out of 195.[10] Unemployment is endemic. There is virtually no health care. The life expectancy at birth is only 48 years. As is the case in many other African countries, school is not an option for children. Less than 34 percent of the population over 15 years of age can read or write.[11]

To walk through most of Freetown or other areas of Sierra Leone is to be inundated with the sights and smells of humans living in miserable conditions. Freetown itself is a chaotic cacophony of car horns, sheet metal shacks, zigzagged dirt roads, street stalls, blaring boomboxes as well as wandering dogs and chickens. Children jump nimbly across water canals full of rotting garbage. These same children play in streets running with filth and human waste. They go home to shacks with no electricity and in most cases, without even four walls. Sometimes the homes are made of trash they have found; they use anything to build something which they can call a home.

In these deplorable conditions, the degree of risk of major infectious diseases is classified as high. Bacterial and protozoal diarrhea, hepatitis A, typhoid fever, malaria, dengue fever, yellow fever, schistosomiasis, rabies, Lassa fever and now Ebola are just some of the diseases you can expect if you have a sip of the wrong water, bite of the wrong food, or can't escape the hordes of mosquitos and other biting insects.

One of the most striking signs of poverty arrives as night falls. Entire portions of the city go dark. You can catch an occasional flicker of candlelight or pulsating orange light from a trashcan fire reflecting off the sides of a tin hut. I was in the Freetown suburb of Waterloo one evening to preach. I was told of a survivor who wanted to tell me and my co-writer, Daniel, his story. We arrived while it was still light but by the time we went to visit the man, we had to find our way in almost total darkness. We could hear voices, but other than that, we were finding our way with the aid of the children who knew their village by heart.

When we arrived at the man's small village hut, it was so dark I could not even see his face. He was standing just two or three feet in front of us, a voice in the darkness telling us his story. The rebels had come to his village and shot him through his head. Suddenly, the flash from Daniel's camera went off and for a bright fraction of a second, I saw this man's face and his fingers pointing to the entrance wound on one side of his head and the exit wound on the other. I could see the small dark bullet scars. It was the only time I saw him and only for a fraction of a second. Then it was dark again.

That darkness of poverty is what the poor of Sierra Leone cannot escape. In the western world, we have a hard time understanding that level of poverty because governments and charitable organizations offer so much assistance. Also, the relative freedom that the West provides holds within it the promise of social mobility. Many who were born in poverty have had the opportunity to rise up to become national leaders and CEOs. Homeless students have graduated from Harvard University. However, there is virtually no help in a country like Sierra Leone. There is no upward mobility. To escape poverty is like trying to escape a black hole. Most simply give up in the face of a system they can never overcome. This is a system that is defined by corruption, specifically during Sierra Leone's pre-war era. Since Sierra Leone became independent from the British in 1961, the government has been dominated by one party or military rule.[12] This created a breeding ground for unchecked corruption. In fact, the government went beyond merely ignoring the needs of its citizens and engaged in actively exploiting them through their rule.[13]

International aid funds were used first to line the pockets of government leaders and their supporters. Then to buy cars, TVs, houses and other luxuries for the leaders. The corruption birthed countless coups led by military and government leaders all wanting their chance to live "the good life." Most of them promised to make reforms but true reforms are hard in the absence of checks and balances. New leaders quickly succumbed to corruption like the rest until they were overthrown themselves.

Africa is full of warlords who have some level of military and civil control, all fighting for different reasons. Some want power, like Uganda's Idi Amin, who killed over 500,000 people. Others want riches, like Liberia's Charles Taylor. Others focus on financing terrorism as Libya's Muammar al-Qaddafi did for many years. Some are ideological while others, like Joseph Kony, the leader of the Lord's Resistance Army which terrorized Uganda, had delusions of establishing a theocratic state. Likewise, Sierra Leone is full of leaders who have used force and violence to push their own agendas. The result was often war.

The massive Cottonwood tree the slaves prayed under in 1792 still stands in the middle of a roundabout in central Freetown. Its base is more than 10 feet wide and towers over nearby buildings. It is believed to be one of the oldest, if not the oldest, cottonwood trees in the world and is still a place where people come to pray. They write down their prayers before stuffing them into the deep trunk crevices and then wait for an answer. This was especially true during the war. The practice rose as a symbol of hope. Christians asked God not to forget Sierra Leone and they wanted God to know they had not forgotten Him. In their darkest days, they could look back to their ancestor's deliverance from the jaws of slavery. And just as the Cottonwood tree still stood strong in those darkest of days, so did their hope of God's deliverance.

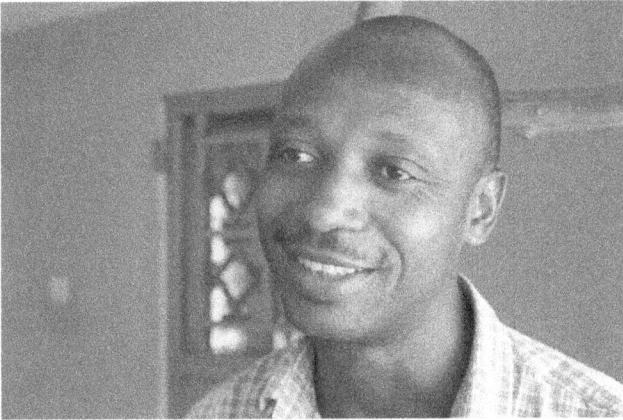

Marah, former Sierra Leone diamond mine worker.

Diamond miner, Kona, Sierra Leone. (credit: USAID)

Diamond miners, Kona. (credit: USAID)

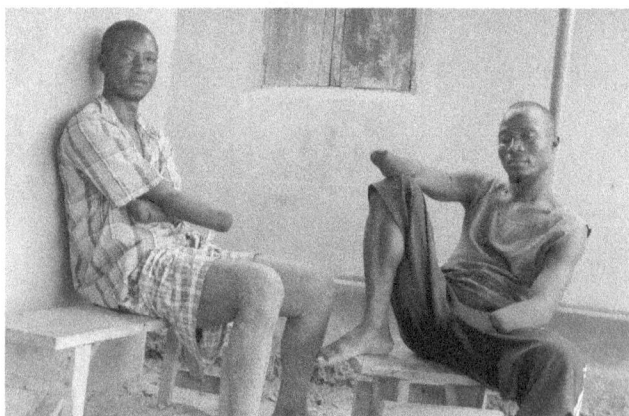

Amputee Village, Waterloo. (credit: Travis Lupick)

Former soldier shows where the bullet went in and where the bullet come out.

The historic Cottonwood tree, Freetown.

3

RUMORS OF WAR

Welcome to Sierra Leone.

If you cannot help us, please do not corrupt us.

BILLBOARD outside Lungi
International Airport, Freetown

"What would an Indian do in Africa?" I asked my Ghanaian friend, Courage. "My work is here in India." I must have asked him that question a hundred times. It was my standard line whenever he told me I needed to come to Ghana and see the work he was doing.

I was living in northern India. My father had moved our family out of southern India to the city of Baroda when I was a boy. He wanted to reach northern India for Christ. Moving from south India to north India was similar to moving to a new country. There were very few Christians and those around us were not receptive to the gospel. In India, there are 15 major languages and over 1,500 sub-dialects, and each state has several languages of its own. We felt the weight of being strangers in a strange land.

Courage must have felt the same way. He came to India from

Ghana to attend college, as many Africans do. When he first arrived in India, Courage realized his wallet and passport had been stolen. He was in a foreign country with no money and no identification. Some of the locals at the train station talked to Courage about his dilemma and realized he was a Christian. Since my father was known in the area for being a Christian, they brought Courage to our house. Courage became part of our family over the next four years. He lived with us during some of that time and eventually graduated from college. He always spoke of going back to Ghana and wanted me to go with him to see the work he would do.

In 2004, I was finally able to make the trip to Ghana to visit Courage and, by God's grace, meet the mayor of Freetown on the flight there. By then, Courage and his wife Confidence were using all their personal resources to reach the Ghanaian people with the gospel. The national election campaign was underway during my visit and after I preached in a remote border village, one of the local parliament members asked me to his home. He told me all about the needs Ghana had and the importance of the upcoming elections. Atta Mills, a Christian, was running as the opposition candidate and had little chance of winning. Then he asked me if I could pray for Professor Atta Mills. Time restrictions prohibited me from meeting with Mills in person, but I spoke with him over the phone and we prayed for several minutes concerning the election and his future role in the government. Although Mills lost in 2004, he was elected president in 2009 and was a successful leader, greatly improving the economy and standard of living.

Years later, I stood on the second-floor balcony of the Gethsemane Evangelical Ministry International in Freetown, Sierra Leone and looked out across the city. My words came back to me: "My work is in India." I began to question why I was there in Africa. Then, the steady beat of a drum from the street interrupted my thoughts. The sound was more like the sound of a hammer against a steel trash can, but it was steady and rhythmic. I looked to see where it was coming from and heard tribal shouts and yells. Looking across the ramshackle rooftops, I caught glimpses of weirdly costumed and masked figures leaping in the streets as crowds followed with cheers. It was a kind of Voodoo dance—a ceremony of one of the animist religious tribes common in West Africa. The dances and festivals revolve around summoning different spirits. In that moment, my heart broke for those people. How could I tell myself that my work was only in India after seeing these lost people who desperately needed to receive the light of the gospel? How could I shut my eyes to West Africa's great need?

Directly to the east of Sierra Leone and four small countries over is the little sliver of a country called Benin. On its coast is the city of Ouidah. Here is the birthplace of Voodoo, the state religion of Benin. Voodoo spread throughout West Africa from Benin until it permeated the tribes of Sierra Leone.

As Christians, we understand the eternal danger of false religions like Voodoo but even in a secular sense, they bring human suffering. Approximately 30 percent of children in Sierra Leone are disabled. Especially in the more rural areas, African religions such as Voodoo teach that disabilities are caused by spirits and magic spells. This belief causes children to be abused, abandoned and even killed. The children who are cast out of families are left to suffer in the streets. A four-year-old girl with cerebral palsy who lived in the rural district of Koinadugu was taken to the village elders by her parents. It was decided the girl was cursed with a magical spell. They were more worried that the spell would infect others in the village than they were for the girl herself. The parents took the girl into the woods and buried her alive.[1]

These religions were not only embraced by RUF, whose fighters welcomed satanic activity, but also by the factions fighting against RUF. The Civil Defense Forces (CDF) were paramilitary organizations made up of different tribes. For the most part, CDF officially supported the government and were anti-RUF, but they were also guilty of terrible acts.

The Kamajors were one of the largest of the CDF forces. They were composed of traditional hunter groups from the Mende tribe in the south and east. The Kamajors believed black magic was the source of their power and would protect them in battle. Wearing bizarre and haunting costumes, they practiced even more bizarre beliefs.

The Kamajor soldiers fortified their bodies with different charms. They performed ritualistic washing before battle and believed that if no non-Kamajors touched them, they would be bullet proof. I spoke with many people who were convinced they witnessed bullets bounce off the skin of these Kamajors. On the battlefield, the Kamajors used guns but also depended on demonic spiritual attacks. Some claimed they controlled bees to aid their attack and were also able to temporarily blind their enemies in order to sneak up on them. They also believed they could change into animals and transport themselves to different parts of the jungle.

A former Kamajor named Jeff who had renounced his former life and became a Christian, spoke with me. That afternoon in Freetown was incredibly hot and to escape the noise of the city, we holed up in a tiny room with the windows shut. It was so hot Daniel's camera and recording equipment shut down. We sat inches from Jeff as he softly and calmly detailed his life as a Kamajor soldier. He and his fellow soldiers would sneak into a village, find a human sacrifice and cook them. Jeff ate their flesh to secure victory in battle.

These animist religions filled a vacuum from what was at that time a dormant Christian church. While the early history of Sierra Leone was dominated by Christianity, its growth went largely defeated by the rise and spread of Islam among the northern tribes beginning in the 18th century. Thirty-five percent of the population was Islamic in 1961 and by 2000, it made up 60 percent of the population. Although today Sierra Leone is a model of religious tolerance and of Christians and Muslims living side by side in peace, it is approximately 70 percent Muslim. The lack of Christianity, the prominence of false religions and the failing infrastructure fostered an apathetic and disaffected youth who were ripe for recruitment by RUF. Sierra Leone's youth were largely illiterate and unemployed. They felt alienated and hopeless. They used drugs and alcohol to disconnect from the grim reality of their daily existence. They certainly had no hope in their government. Aside from farming, the other common option for the youth was to work in the brutal diamond mines. Their resentment towards the government and society in general was steadily growing.

Much of their resentment is understandable. Though the slaves who landed in what would be Freetown were indeed free, Sierra Leone was a British protectorate until 1961. Great Britain discovered many resources in Sierra Leone worth "protecting" back in the 1880s and agreed to do so, even if the locals didn't want their protection or government. After Sierra Leone's independence in 1961, there were a few and fleeting brief years of democratic rule. Siaka Stevens was elected president in 1967. He briefly lost power in a coup but was then reinstated through another coup. African politics are often compared to the weather: if you don't like who's in charge, wait about 5 minutes.

Stevens' 17-year reign is now known as the "17-Year Plague of Locusts." In a few short years, he took a functioning multi-partied democracy and turned it into a one-party state. He pushed through a new Constitution outlawing any dissent to his party, the All Peoples Congress or APC. Dissidents were rounded up and disappeared. Innocent Sierra Leone citizens were accused and convicted as needed.

Stevens used the diamonds of Sierra Leone for his own personal wealth and as payment to his loyalists. He joined forces with Jamil Sahid Mohamed Khalil, a Lebanese-Sierra Leonean who became one of the richest men in all of Africa by exporting diamonds illegally to Antwerp. While Stevens was unable to engage in commerce as president, Jamil certainly could. The extent of profit from their illegal selling of diamonds grew so fast and quick that by November 3, 1969, after only 2 years in office, $3.4 million of one month of government diamond production disappeared into the pockets of Stevens and Khalil.[2]

Before APC had taken control of the mines, the diamond trade was one-third of the Sierra Leone GDP and contributed 70 percent of Sierra Leone's foreign exchange reserves. Twenty-five years later, less than $100,000 worth of diamonds made it through proper legal channels. The day Stevens stepped down, Sierra Leone had only $196,000 in foreign reserves while he was $500 million richer.

Stevens appointed Major General Saidu Momoh as his successor. Momoh promised reforms and a corruption-free government, but the situation only deteriorated. Government workers ransacked offices for anything they could find and sell so they could feed their families. The government also stopped paying teachers, which destroyed the educational system. Sierra Leonean citizens witnessed lawless government leaders who, even if they were caught, were rarely charged and if charged, rarely convicted. If by chance they were convicted, they never went to jail.

Sierra Leone was a "kleptocracy" and a "shadow state." Each new regime committed atrocities that were worse than the previous one. There was zero accountability and all dissent was crushed. The immense failure of leaders such as Stevens and Momoh tilled the soil for complete social breakdown and the future civil war. By the beginnings of the war in 1991, Sierra Leone was a divided society suffering from vast inequality and primed for violence and war. As if that were not bad enough, Sierra Leone's neighbor to the east, Liberia, was fighting a Ghaddafi-funded rebellion that started in 1989 and was led by Charles Taylor and his disciple and later founder of RUF, Foday Sanko.

It is safe to say that the Sierra Leone Civil War would not have happened if not for Charles Taylor and his terrorist army, the National Patriotic Front of Liberia. It was no secret he was a violent man. In 1997, he famously ran for president on the campaign slogan, "He kill my ma, he kill my pa, but I will vote for him." Taylor's rebellion in Liberia was as violent and brutal as the civil war he would instigate in Sierra Leone. Among his favorite tactics were the cutting off limbs, using child soldiers, cannibalism, torture and rape. Overall, more than 250,000 people died.[3]

Taylor became infuriated with Sierra Leone when they based the West African intervention force ECOMOG (The Economic Community of West African States Monitoring Group) at Lungi International Airport outside Freetown and used it to stage bombing runs on Taylor's forces. Taylor went on the radio and declared that Sierra Leone would "taste the bitterness of war." He used his anger to direct Foday Sanko to begin RUF operations in Sierra Leone in 1991. Taylor promised to pay and arm Sanko. In return, Sanko promised Taylor diamonds.[4] Sanko was true to his promise and reportedly sent back mayonnaise jars full of diamonds. By the time of his eventual capture and arrest, Charles Taylor's wealth was estimated to be close to half a billion US dollars.[5]

Founder of Grace Evangelical Ministry (GEM), Dr. Sidikiee & his wife with Brother Bennie in Freetown, Sierra Leone.

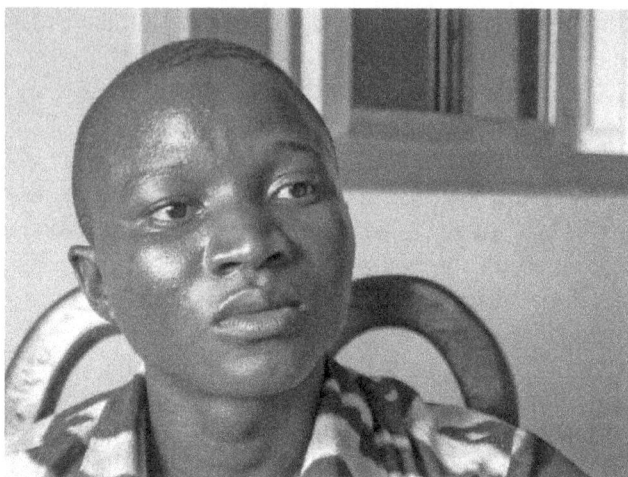

Jeff, former Kamajor soldier.

Children in front of their home in Freetown.

Brother Bennie with village children, outside of Freetown.

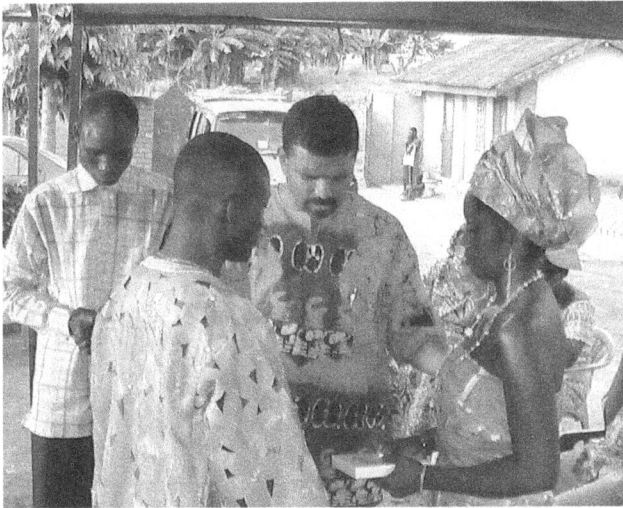

Brother Bennie's first visit to Ghana, West Africa for Courage and Confidence's wedding.

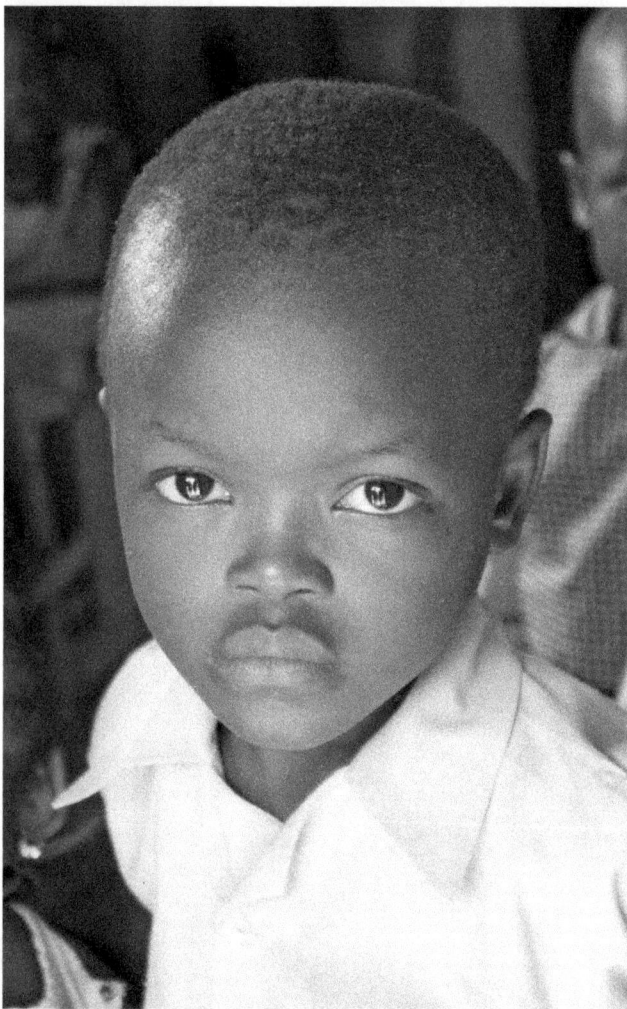

Will this child have a future free of war and oppression?
Let us pray.

4

UNFORTUNATELY, I MET WITH THEM

Children played guessing games, telling each
other whether the gun fired was an AK-47, a G3,
an RPG or a machine gun.

ISHMAEL BEAH,
A Long Way Gone: Memoirs of a Boy Soldier [1]

I t was 2010, and I had just returned to my home in Virginia after a month-long trip to India. I got a call from an old friend, Pastor Henry Pitts Evans. He told me how the Lord had impressed upon his heart that I should accompany him to Sierra Leone to preach at a crusade. I jokingly said, "Man, you have the wrong person. I don't preach in crusades. Maybe you've got another friend named Bennie?"

Pastor Henry laughed. "Bennie, I'm getting the tickets and you are coming."

To be polite, I told him I needed to consult with my wife before I made such a decision. But Lina could overhear our conversation and immediately said, "Bennie, I have said time and again, you don't have to bring me into these ministerial decisions. I will never say no to you answering God's call. You know the rules so just do it! Whatever the Lord says, do it." I was hoping when I told her why I said no she would back me up. I was wrong. "Bennie, if God opens a door, you need to go." She had told me this on more than one occasion in the past, and she was always right. So, what could I do? I packed for Sierra Leone. I remembered my conversation with the mayor of Freetown six years earlier and his invitation to come to Sierra Leone. I was disappointed to find that I had somehow misplaced his card and could not remember his contact information.

Just a few days later, our plane flew over Sierra Leone. I looked down on the carpeted jungle and the small dotted villages. I tried to imagine what it was like as the war began back in 1991 and RUF came bursting through the jungle bringing various forms of violence with them. Foday Sanko and his troops invaded on the eastern border Sierra Leone shares with Liberia. Foday started with only about 100 fighters made up of Sierra Leonean dissidents, Liberian fighters and some mercenaries from Burkina Faso. The first place they invaded was the city of Bomaru in the Kailahun district.

At the time, most Sierra Leoneans had no idea what RUF was. Sometimes, they didn't even know the name of the attacking force until a soldier carved the initials "RUF" onto the victim's chests with a machete. A minority of Sierra Leoneans had a vague idea that RUF wanted to overthrow the corrupt and incompetent government, which meant RUF had some initial support but only before news of their atrocities began to spread.

RUF came roaring into villages in old battered jeeps and cars packed with armed soldiers hanging off the sides. They brandished machetes and machine guns. Many of them were just boys and some were so small they dragged their machine guns on the ground. They would only lift them long enough to kill a villager.

One of the main goals of RUF at that time was to disrupt the upcoming Sierra Leone elections. The government wanted to make sure everyone voted, so they coined the phrase, "One Hand, One Vote." Unfortunately, RUF turned that slogan into a cruel reason to chop off the hands of would-be voters. If they took both hands then there would be no vote. The amputated victims were cruelly mocked and ordered to march to Freetown and show their stumps to President Momoh.

Serry Kargbo was a former Muslim and had been a Christian for two years when RUF invaded his village. Soldiers rounded up the villagers while others burned every single house to the ground but not before taking everything of value. As in other villages, the rebels demanded that the people join forces with them. The RUF force was still small at that time and needed all the soldiers, porters and sex slaves it could get. Anyone who refused had two options: have their arms or feet chopped off or have a nail driven through their lips while having their fingers chopped off. After witnessing over 100 of his family and fellow villagers suffer these cruelties, Serry relented and volunteered as a porter for RUF.

Edward Conteh and his eight children had been on the run for three days, hiding from the rebels who came to his village and started killing indiscriminately. His children, weary and thirsty, said, "Father, we need to go fetch water." He told them, "No, it is not safe. I'll go and fetch water." Edward then joined a group of other villagers who had fled and made his way to get water for his children. As he shared his story with me, his eyes grew sad and he said, "Unfortunately, I met with them."

The rebels emerged from the bush and caught the villagers by surprise. They killed every one of them except Edward. He stood alone around the bodies. Then, the rebels put guns to both sides and the back of his head and forced him to lie down on the ground among the bodies. They commanded him to put his hands out so they could chop them off. Edward made the choice to live as an amputee instead of not living at all.[2] They used an axe. It took, at least, five blows to complete the amputation.

The estimation is that 27,000 Sierra Leoneans suffered a similar fate during the civil war. Amputees are a common site throughout the entire country. When you see someone missing a limb, you do not wonder how they lost it. You just know.

Although amputation is the atrocity most commonly linked to the Sierra Leone Civil War, the rebels spent their time devising many other horrific ways to inflict torture. They would often force children to engage in sexual acts with their family members in public. If they refused, they were killed. They would herd villagers together, lock them in a hut and burn them alive. They would bury people alive or roast them over fires on spits.

Serry, who had joined RUF to carry their supplies, told us what happened to him over the weeks that followed:

> The rebels used to walk 40 miles a day making us to carry the load, if anyone of us complained about tiredness then they would say that you'll retire forever and shoot or cut the feet. Some 10 people got killed because they complained. So, fearing death, we all suffered the load without complaining.
>
> They were taking us to Freetown. On the way, they saw a pregnant woman going to her village from the forest. These rebels, six of them, suddenly started arguing among themselves whether the woman was pregnant with a baby boy or a girl. So they decided to cut the woman's stomach and find out. They caught the woman and cut her stomach only to find out that it was a baby girl. Leaving the dead mother and the fetus to die, the rebels moved ahead on their course. As we were still not able to remove the memory of the slain mother and her fetus, the rebels caught three young girls from the outskirts of the next village. All six of the rebels went in turns to rape those three girls in front of us. After they satisfied their evil appetite of sex, they took the

girls along with them for future entertainment.

On this horrifying journey, we came across another small village called Kabassa. The rebels attacked it, looting their valuables and also asked them to join their mutiny. But some refused. Angered by their refusal and to teach the villagers a lesson, they [tortured the villagers] and told them to call the president to come and release them from this.

The rebels continued to Freetown, creating havoc wherever they crossed. There was another village called Kamahayibo. Now this village had animal hunters who were skilled in hunting wild animals. They got the news of the rebels coming and decided to fight the rebels. As we approached near the village, they launched an attack on us, but unfortunately the rebels overpowered them and killed 30 of the villagers by bullets. Then they threw 40 of the villagers in the well including small children and women. They captured around 30 people and took them with their valuables to Freetown.

Kamalu, a small village, came on our way but the villagers ran away, hearing of the rebels. Five small children were left behind. The rebels took those children and threw them into the nearby river. We stayed there for one day.

The next day the rebels took all of us and started the painful journey. We came across a very small village with only 5 houses. Now it had been 20 days already with these merciless raiders. I acquired their confidence that I will not escape because they used to send me to the village to get some goats or sheep to eat and every time I returned. But this time, I was having something *else in my mind. Again, I got the orders to go and find something to eat. I went, never to return. God helped me and I was successful to escape to my hometown after almost a month.*[3]

The rebels added to their numbers by taking children, some as young as seven years old and turning them into soldiers. If they didn't trust them with a gun, they made them porters. Girls served as sex slaves. Since children were smaller and harder to see, the rebels used many of them as ambushers.

The RUF quickly grew in size, largely through their recruitment of youth. Some youth joined willingly though the overwhelming disillusionment they had in their government, country and life in general. There was also an abundance of youth in Sierra Leone at the time as a result of the First Liberian Civil War when 80,000 refugees had fled to the Sierra Leone border. A large portion of these refugees were youth who were easily captured at refugee camps. These youth were often starving and needed medical help. RUF made any promises they needed to make to get them to join.

Once the youth joined, many of them began to enjoy the unlimited sense of power they possessed in the taking of human lives. In a sense, joining RUF gave a greater sense of purpose to many of the children than anything else in their normal day to day lives ever did.

Even so, most were forced at the barrel of a gun or the sharp edge of a machete. The child soldiers would be brainwashed right away. They were forced to kill their parents or their friends. By some estimates, children made up between 40 and 50 percent of RUF's total force of about 15,000.

Idrissa was a young boy when he was forced to watch RUF rebels beat his father to death while his uncle was shot and killed. He ran with the remaining survivors to hide in a church with a local pastor. They slept there that night. They awoke the next morning to find RUF rebels had surrounded the church. The pastor bravely went out to reason with them and save the lives of those inside.

He was killed. The rebels then stormed the church. Idrissa's aunt fled but was gunned down. Inside, the survivors were randomly separated; some to die and some to live. Idrissa saw a moment of opportunity and fled through a window. He heard gunshots and felt a sharp pain in his leg. He hobbled into the jungle as quickly as he could. He had been shot, but he survived only to be caught and forced into being a child soldier a short time later. They took him into a nearby forest along with 70 others and trained them. If anyone refused an order or tried to escape, they were killed on the spot. They were supplied with alcohol, marijuana and even heroin. They were psychologically broken and desensitized.

Once trained, the rebels forced Idrissa and the others to march toward Freetown. On the way, they came across the school that Idrissa and many of the other child soldiers had once attended. One of Idrissa's friends, Sorrie, refused to attack his former school; he was immediately shot and killed. Sorrie had been the former head boy of that school before being part of RUF's child soldier army. At that moment, Idrissa and some of the other child soldiers turned and began firing at the rebels. The rebels fired back, and chaos broke out. Idrissa fled into a cemetery and waited out the fight with five others. They were later captured at a checkpoint and held in a small room. When the rebels arrived, they hacked the other five children to death but left Idrissa. He still can not understand why they left him alive. He believes it was God.

The true horror of being a child soldier is difficult to comprehend. The following is a condensed testimony of a child soldier testifying at the United Nations Special Court for Sierra Leone (SCSL) after the war:

> *Prosecutor: Do you know what group captured you and the other boys and girls in Koinadugu town?*
>
> *Witness: Yes. Both AFRC and RUF because they would mark us with their names.*

Pros: What kind of training did you receive in the bush?

Wit: They showed us how to crawl in the bush and how to dismantle and clean guns.

Pros: How old were you when this happened?

Wit: 12 years old.

Pros: Did anything else happen?

Wit: 55 and O5 [Commander nicknames] ordered that all the boys be trained. Kabila and Mohammed helped train us and he gave me two blue tablets.

Pros: Did you experience any feelings after you took those tablets?

Wit: My eyes were red and I started feeling "bold."

Pros: What group did Kabila, your commander, belong to?

Wit: He marked me RUF on my chest. Then, I knew he was RUF.

Pros: What happened after you took the two blue pills?

Wit: 55 told us to loot and kill the people in the village. We went to a house with five people: two men, a woman and two children. Kabila demonstrated to us how to do it and hacked the first man on his neck. I then hacked the woman next to him and hacked her on her chest and her side. I also hacked the child with her. I hacked the woman on the back of her neck and on her breast with a machete. I hacked the child on his neck and on his side. One of them begged me not to do it but Kabila told me to do it or he would kill me.

So, I hacked him as well and cut off his head. Some of the fighters on the other side were looting and burning down houses. Then, we left.

Pros: What happened next?

Wit: There was a White priest who was captured, and we went into the forest and heard heavy fighting. Then, we laid down in that forest because we were told to do so.

Pros: Did you perform any role?

Wit: I carried ammunition for Kabila and I had my machete.

Pros: Were you forced to carry anything else?

Wit: Sometimes, he would give me the gun but it was heavy for me so he took it away from me. Kabila brought marijuana and I smoked it until I started vomiting.

Pros: Prior to this time, had you ever smoked a cigarette?

Wit: No, that was my first-time smoking anything.

Pros: Did anything happen next?

Wit: Camba ordered his boys (Bazuh and another) to capture one girl. They put her into a house and Camba raped her. John was standing outside as the bodyguard. We stayed in that village looting and taking things and then left.

Pros: You were 12 years of age at the time. How would you describe the ages of the boys you were trained with.

Wit: Some were older than me and others were the same age as me.

Pros: What happened next?

Wit: I met with Kabila and he told me that he was given an order by his boss, Musa. This order was to go to Freetown and we were to overthrow the government that was in power. We should not loot or kill. Kabila said that won't work but kill everything including goats, sheep, everything. He said, "Spare no soul."

Pros: What happened next?

Wit: We walked during the night. In the morning, we found a forest where we would stay during the day and then walk during the night. We were going to Freetown.[4]

Idrissa, former child soldier with the RUF.

Former child soldier.

Burned down school, Freetown. (credit: USAID)

Freetown, Sierra Leone (credit: Random Institute)

Steve and Brother Bennie at the presidential home with First Lady, Ernestine Mills.

Young woman of Freetown.

5

SURVIVING THE "RESCUERS"

WE YU MƐN LƐPƐT, YU NƆ FƆ
VƐKS WE I DE IT YU GOT. (Sherbro)
When you raise a leopard, you shouldn't
be upset when it eats your goat.

KRIO PROVERB

A t the center of all the horror and mayhem was Foday Sanko, the RUF leader and Sierra Leone national who was trained and backed by Charles Taylor and Gaddafi. Compared to his notorious reputation, Foday's past seemed innocuous. He was a former army corporal and a television cameraman. As a student leader, he joined the Sierra Leone army and was arrested in 1969 for being involved in a coup attempt. He was jailed for ten years and released in 1980. He later lost his job as a cameraman after once again speaking out against the government and in 1982 he left Sierra Leone for Libya. Alongside other disgruntled Sierra Leone expats there, the revolutionary ideas of Gaddafi began to take root. By the time he left Libya to take part in Charles Taylor's rebellion in Liberia, he had been completely radicalized.

Some Sierra Leonean's say that Foday Sanko was "religious". He claimed to be a Christian, although it cannot possibly be true. But that's often the case in Africa. It has been stated that those in Africa take their religion everywhere, including the battlefield. Not that this was a religious war. But religion in Africa is deeply ingrained. African life is "anchored in religion whether it be the individual's relationship to the family, the clan and tribe, or morality, law, worship, politics, social status, economics, etiquette, wars and peace."[1]

RUF developed its own religion through the course of the war. It started with elements of African Traditional Religions but later integrated elements of Christianity and Islam. Prayer, including the Lord's Prayer, was compulsory every morning at 6 AM. Soldiers often wore crosses and rosaries alongside their magical charms.

But it wasn't only RUF that was praying in the jungles of Sierra Leone. There was an array of factions and sides in the war. In fact, many of the youth who did not want to join RUF used their anger to join other factions. Jeff, the Kamajor-turned-Christian pastor, was just 15 years old when he was captured from his village along with his brother. Jeff was able to escape but his brother was not. So, Jeff followed the RUF rebel group holding his brother, hiding in the dense leaves off the trail and waiting for the right moment to free him. At one point, the rebels stopped and confronted Jeff's brother, demanding he join them or die. He told the rebels he would not kill anyone, so he refused to join them. Jeff watched as his brother was shot to death. It was then that Jeff decided to join the Kamajors and start fighting RUF with an AK-47.

For many, the Kamajors were as bad as the rebels. The town of Kabala was supposed to be protected by these warriors who, in turn, were going to be given housing and supplies by the Sierra Leone government. When the rebels moved in to attack Kabala, the civilians called out for help from the Kamajors, but most of them had moved on because they weren't being supplied by the government. The few who did show up did not have ammo.

Some of the survivors of other attacks who had fled into Kabala began to accuse the Kamajors of joining RUF and conspiring to defeat the town. One evening, the whole town gathered to sacrifice a red goat and hopefully reveal the identity of the traitor. At that exact moment, the first rocket-propelled grenades exploded in the city. Finding the traitor would have to wait.

Since the few Kamajors that remained had no ammunition, everyone began to run for the jungle. The RUF left after they had burned down 200 houses and killed, at least, 100 people. About an hour later, the Sierra Leone Army (SLA) finally arrived. The survivors showed them the direction the rebels fled. Though the RUF couldn't have gotten far, the SLA refused to go after the rebels. They simply turned around and went back to Freetown.

Marah, the former diamond miner I spoke with in Freetown, was working in a mine in Tongo under the direction of RUF when the Kamajors suddenly attacked and routed the RUF forces. Unfortunately, those Kamajors suspected many of the civilian diamond mine workers to be rebels and immediately killed 500 of them. They told the survivors, including Marah, to leave as quickly as they could. As the survivors tried to flee, another group of Kamajors attacked them. They took all their belongings and forced them into slave labor on a coffee farm.

The Kamajors still suspected many of the captured civilians to be rebels. Just two weeks into his slave labor, Marah, his uncle and 350 others, were forced to line up in a field. Marah's uncle was called out and shot for supposedly being a rebel. As if that was not horrific enough, the Kamajors decided they would make an example out of Marah's uncle to anyone who refused to confess. They took out his liver, cooked and ate it in front of all of them.

Again, Marah and the others were ordered to confess they were rebels. There was only silence. None of them were RUF rebels. Nevertheless, the Kamajors began shooting the men one by one. Seven men were killed before they reached Marah. He pleaded his innocence to them. Instead of shooting him they began to beat him with iron bars. As he felt his life beginning to fade, he cried out to God to save him. That was when a respected Kamajor woman ran up to the group. She told them he was not a rebel and that he was only there to work in the mine as a civilian. His life was saved. Unfortunately, Marah still had to survive the other "rescuers" of the Sierra Leone civilians—ECOMOG and AFRC soldiers—who later killed his sister and disappeared with her son, who was never seen again.

ECOMOG, The Economic Community of West African States Monitoring Group, was a West African multilateral armed force established by the Economic Community of West African States (ECOWAS). Basically, ECOMOG was a formal arrangement for separate armies to work together but the bulk of the fighting force was made up of Nigerian soldiers. Other soldiers came from Guinea-Bissau, Sierra Leone, The Gambia, Liberia, Mali, Burkina Faso, and Niger.

Corruption and looting was so common among ECOMOG soldiers that the acronym became known as "Every Car or Movable Object Gone."[2] The ECOMOG soldiers routinely committed atrocities against the very people they were supposed to protect. A United Nations human rights mission charged the soldiers with summarily executing dozens of civilians. They issued a report describing systematic rights violations by the "peacekeeping" troops. There were documented cases of ECOMOG forces bombing civilian targets, shooting at human shields and mistreating staff of various NGOs and aid organizations like the Red Cross.[3]

Idrissa, the child soldier who escaped during the schoolhouse fight, was being transported in a truck by the SLA (Sierra Leone Army) to their headquarters in Freetown. The convoy came under attack by RUF. The civilians fled the convoy and most wound up at a ferry crossing by a bridge. About 400 people were lined up on that bridge to use the ferry and cross into Freetown. Suddenly, Idrissa heard a commotion further up the bridge towards the ferry. The ECOMOG solders had discovered a woman hiding a pistol between her and her baby strapped on her back. Now, the peacekeeping force of soldiers were worried that RUF soldiers might be hiding among the civilians. The soldiers decided to kill all 400 people on the bridge just in case any of them were soldiers.

Idrissa told me, "As the ECOMOG were preparing to kill us, they told us to say our last prayers. For the first time, I called on Jesus from the bottom of my heart as we were all praying and crying for our loved ones. I got the boldness to ask the [SLA] commander for a Bible and, to my surprise, the commander permitted me to go and take it. There was this big building just in front of us. It was the base camp for the ECOMOG soldiers. I was told to go there and get the Bible. I went inside the room and opened the Bible to the Book of Revelation 3:20: Jesus says, 'Behold I stand at the door and knock it. If anyone hears my voice and opens the door, I will come and dine with him.' This word touched my heart and it gave me courage to run from the building. There were no guards at the back of the building and I ran from there to the forest where I hid myself for one week."

Many others on the bridge did not survive. ECOMOG soldiers shot countless civilians and dumped their bodies over the bridge into the water. Many Sierra Leoneans began to hate the Nigerian peacekeeping soldiers.

ECOMOG troops had been called in to fight RUF alongside SLA, since SLA was basically a ceremonial army. They had never fought a large war at home and the vast majority of these soldiers had never seen combat. It quickly became apparent that SLA was completely unprepared to fight RUF.

Morale among SLA soldiers was also incredibly low. The government could not pay the troops and could not afford to equip them properly. Still, they sent them into the jungle and expected them to fight off RUF. They did not want to fight them directly so they would search for rebels among the civilian population, resulting in countless deaths. Survivors of RUF attacks would often have to face SLA's "clean up" operations in which they were sent to concentration camps to separate possible rebels from society. After they were gone, SLA troops would take everything they owned.

As a result, more disaffected Sierra Leoneans joined the RUF cause. SLA soldiers became known as Sobels, or soldiers by day and rebels by night. By 1993, two years into the war, the two sides were hard to tell apart. Helpless citizens were terrified of turning to military personnel, fearing they would be killed by the ones meant to protect them. This was one of the main reasons why RUF was winning so quickly in the first few years of the war. As early as October 1991, it was clear SLA was losing to a group that had started with about 100 fighters only eight months earlier. By early 1992, RUF began seizing diamond mines and driving out the local population. It added forced recruits to their army, giving RUF the financial means they needed to keep their operations going.

The low morale among SLA soldiers led to a coup in April 1992 by a young officer named Valentine Strasser. He had warned President Momoh of the low morale in the army. Momoh could see the writing on the wall and fled his office, leaving behind a few troops to guard the government. Strasser's soldiers easily overtook the guards. They seized the government radio station and Strasser declared himself the head of state. At the time and at 25 years old, Strasser was the youngest head of state in the world.

President Momoh was deposed. The parliament was dissolved and all political parties were banned. Another acronymed organization was added—the NPRC or National Provincial Ruling Council.

Strasser, who claimed to be a Christian, immediately declared a national week of fasting and prayer in order to end the war. He declared himself "The Redeemer" who would cleanse Sierra Leone's politics and bring peace. He tried to set up peace talks with Foday Sanko and RUF, but Foday rejected every offer.

Under Strasser, SLA gained ground against RUF. By March 1993, they had pushed them all the way back to the Liberian border. Meanwhile, Taylor's National Patriotic Front forces were under attack in Liberia, preventing RUF from getting the supplies they desperately needed. There was hope RUF would be completely defeated by the end of 1993. However, the government's poor treatment of their SLA soldiers caught up with them once again. Far from Freetown, in the diamond mining districts, the soldiers began helping themselves to all the diamonds they could find. They also decided to earn money by selling guns and ammunition to the rebels in exchange for cash. The pro-government Kamajors and other CDF forces tried to prevent SLA from looting and selling arms and wound up engaging them in battles. But Strasser and his party, the NPRC, had reasons for the war to drag on. As long as the country was at war, he and his military party would hold on to power. As soon as war ended, democratic elections would be held. So for the NPRC, as long as the war was far from Freetown, there was no real urgency to stamp it out.

All that changed in January 1995 when RUF forces staged a comeback and seized bauxite and rutile mines in the southwest. This choked the country's finances and enabled an advance that would put them only twenty miles outside Freetown. Christians in Sierra Leone watched as the government failed in every attempt to bring the war to an end. They had little faith in the government overall, but with each RUF victory, their sense of urgency grew. The circumstances began to push them to seek God as they never had before. This was the beginning of the transformation of the church in Sierra Leone.

———

Christians became absolutely convinced that only the supernatural intervention of God would end the war. The church saw the civil war as a spiritual battle so church leaders developed their strategy accordingly. They fought spiritually through prayer and fasting. Pastors across the country began to call on their congregations to fast and pray. The Council of Churches in Sierra Leone (CCSL) sent out specific times of prayer so that all Christians could pray at the same time.

Outside of Freetown, some church leaders had been killed though it is difficult to say if they had been killed specifically because they were Christians. Many had been kidnapped including Freetown's Roman Catholic archbishop, Joseph Henry Ganda. He survived, but his fellow captives were killed. An Italian priest and nun were shot. The priest survived his wounds, but the nun died. A Kenyan and Bangladeshi nun were killed together, but it remains unclear if they were killed by RUF or ECOMOG troops.

Other pastors under constant attack in the remote areas of Sierra Leone had no churches left. The buildings had been burned to the ground and their flock either had been slaughtered or scattered; some going further in the country or to the refugee camps in Ghana and Guinea. Many of the pastors took their families and fled as well. (An important fact to keep in mind is that these pastors weren't fleeing persecution. This was not a religious war. There are no documented instances where anyone was killed specifically because he or she was a Christian. It may have happened but if it did, it was exceedingly rare.) Once the pastors arrived in the refugee camps, they immediately went about setting up churches within the camps. This resulted in untold numbers of conversions within the refugee camps which were a mix of Muslims and practitioners of African Traditional Religions.

Many other pastors stayed behind, ministering, preaching and delivering Bibles. James Farmer was a Sierra Leonean who worked for Gideon International during the war. He even took Bibles to the rebels in the bush. I asked him if he was scared. He just laughed and said no, he was sharing the Word of God which was the only way for the rebels to truly change. He discovered many of the rebels wanted preaching because they had already grown weary of the life they were living.

One rebel took a Bible and slipped it into his shirt pocket. A while later when James saw the same rebel. He ran up to James and exclaimed how he had been shot, but the Bible in his shirt pocket had stopped the bullet.

Dr. Patrick George of Gethsemane Evangelical Ministry International was a resident of Freetown. He made several trips out into the country to preach and minister during the war. He said,

"I preached courage, hope and salvation." Sometimes, the sound of gunfire would erupt as he was preaching to an already nervous crowd. Some of the churches he preached in were eventually attacked and Christians killed. It was a struggle, he confesses. How could the hope he preached overcome the atrocities they experienced?

Brother Bennie greeted by Pastor Sunil at his church outside of Freetown.

Brother Bennie with residents of Pastor Sunil's Children's Home.

Steve with the children at the new school building built in Sierra Leone.

6

I DON'T CARE

There's more to doing good than hating evil.

ANONYMOUS

I woke up in Freetown and wept.

I had finally arrived in Sierra Leone the night before. I was still jet-lagged from my previous trip to India, but thankfully, my wife had convinced me to come. Lungi International Airport sits across the bay from Freetown in the coastal town of Lungi. You can get to Freetown by road, but that is a three-hour bumpy ride. The alternative is a 45-minute speedboat ride, so I rode the speedboat and crossed the harbor at night.

After so many years and stories, I was ready to see Sierra Leone. I tried to make out Freetown and the buildings but with so few lights on at night, it is difficult to see anything. The next morning looked out of my window and the morning light revealed the vast poverty.

I saw men and women with no hands, and sometimes, no feet. I saw the scars of war across their bodies, across the landscape, and across the soul of the people. War orphans begged in the streets. My heart was broken. I was in tears. I could not believe what I was seeing, and this was from a man who grew up in India and saw intense poverty his entire life. This was not my first time to a poor area or country. I wasn't a student on my first mission trip. Yet, I was deeply broken by the misery of the people and their need for the gospel of Jesus Christ.

While seeing and understanding the situation in Freetown, my conversation with the mayor of Freetown came to mind. I could not recall his name, but I had a vague memory of how he looked. I wanted to see the mayor I had met on my flight to Ghana years earlier, but my chief concern was preaching the gospel. My thoughts were consumed with trying to figure out what to preach in this broken land. I tried to prepare and found myself in the same situation as my friend, Dr. Patrick George, the wartime preacher. What do I preach when what I am saying—a message of hope and salvation—is so different from what these people are experiencing? I knew that God and His gospel would save. My trust was in Him, but I knew I had to be prepared.

Dr. Patrick George introduced me to a pastor named Dr. Sidikie. This pastor worked in the Freetown hospital during the war. He treated casualties in the emergency room. When a victim would come in, they had no way of notifying their families. So, Dr. Sidikie would risk his life and go out to find the family so they could know what was happening.

Pastor Henry arranged a leadership meeting and I shared what the Lord was doing on the frontline. It is always exciting to speak in African churches. They are very responsive and their engagement boosts your spirit.

Dr. George and Dr. Sidikie drove me to a small village literally named *I Don't Care*. Even the name of the town revealed the desperation of the people. They had given up.

It was night and completely dark by the time we arrived in I-Don't-Care. There were no lights in the village. Dr. George told me that the government had tried to install streetlights in the town but the villagers tore them down. They wanted it dark. By the time we reached I-Don't-Care, it was pitch black outside with a vast sea of stars above, which you could never see anywhere near a city. The vehicle stopped in front of a mosque and we saw dim lamps shining in people's homes. I could hear a P.A. system and singing from a long way off, but as we drew closer to the mosque, I realized the meeting was behind the mosque itself.

The only lights were generator-powered lights focused on a small platform where we would be preaching. I looked past the lights and saw that I would be preaching right in front of the mosque. While I wasn't surprised to see a mosque (Sierra Leone did have more Muslims than Christians), I admit I was nervous for a moment. There would be many Muslims in the audience. Would they accept my message?

To see the Christians of I-Don't-Care dancing and praising God adjacent to the mosque was beautiful. As I was led to the stage, I remembered the words of David from 2 Samuel 7:18, "Who am I, Sovereign LORD, and what is my family, that you have brought me this far and counted me worthy to stand and proclaim your name among the multitudes." How humbling to be on the receiving end of such a great honor. I was in tears.

As I shared, the Lord brought to mind the incident of meeting the mayor on a flight to Ghana. When I told that story, some of the people were giggling though I knew it wasn't just a funny line. I continued by sharing my testimony about what the Lord had done in my life and ended by asking the people to give their lives to Jesus. That evening, over sixty men and women came to the altar to receive Jesus Christ as their personal Lord and Savior. I was in tears and sobbing like a child, incapable of speech as I witnessed God's saving grace.

When I finished preaching, I sat down. A few ladies from the crowd came over to me.

"Sir, do you know the mayor's name?" They asked.

"I believe it was Williams, Mayor Williams," I replied.

They gasped and started doing a little African celebratory

dance. I had no idea what was going on.

"Sir, do you see that house there with the light on?"

I looked down the street to where they were pointing and saw the only other light anywhere close by, in front of a house.

"That is the mayor's house! You are preaching in front of the mayor's house!"

I could not believe it. After all this time, God had brought me to Sierra Leone and right in front of the mayor's house. The village pastor got excited and told me I absolutely had to meet the mayor. People started praising God. They knew the mayor was not in town at the time, but he was due to return in two days. Unfortunately, we were scheduled to travel to the Kono District to conduct more crusades.

━━━━━━━

Villages like I-Don't-Care were continually abandoned and then re-inhabited during the war. In 1995, as RUF rebels were about 20 miles from Freetown, people fled from village to village trying to outrun and escape the rebels. It became a cat-and-mouse game of fleeing each village as it became consumed, burned to the ground and the villagers killed.

At this time, Strasser knew his NPRC was outmatched by the reinvigorated RUF. He needed to take desperate measures. He reached out to a group called Executive Outcomes (EO), a mercenary force based in South Africa. Strasser quickly worked out an agreement with EO to fight RUF in exchange for $1.8 million a month.

Strasser also made a deal with the Canadian mining company, DiamondWorks Ltd. Once EO gained control over the diamond mines, DiamondWorks would come in and mine using local labor and give the government 37.5% of their net profits.[1] These profits would go towards paying EO.

EO set out on three objectives: to defeat RUF, regain control of the diamond mines and destroy RUF headquarters. In the months that followed, EO proved themselves more than a match for RUF. In only 10 days, EO used highly skilled soldiers and sophisticated operations to push the rebel forces 60 miles back all the way to the interior of the country. It only took seven months—and help from the loyal factions of SLA and the Kamajors—to recapture the major diamond mining districts and the critical RUF base in Kangari Hills. RUF forces were devastated and were finally ready to admit defeat and sign a peace agreement.

With Freetown secure, Strasser was ready to implement his promise of free elections. He proclaimed that there would be free elections in March 1996, but he had a problem. When he gained control of Sierra Leone only 3 days after his 25th birthday in 1992, he became the world's youngest head of state. However, Sierra Leone's constitution stated that presidential candidates had to be at least 45 years of age. Strasser tried to change the constitutional age for a presidential candidate from 45 to 30 so he could be a candidate and continue his reign. But this sudden change was his undoing and Strasser was thrown out by a coup led by his deputy, Brigadier General Julius Bio.

The coup left Executive Outcomes in an unstable position. They threatened to leave the country if elections were not held by March 1996, as Strasser had promised. Julius Bio resisted at first. But knowing fully well the need for EO's continued presence, he finally agreed and the process of holding free elections began. In the meantime, Bio met with Foday Sanko in Abidjan, Côte d'Ivoire in February 1996. A two-month cease-fire was declared by RUF. But at the same time, they rejected the upcoming election which Foday thought was a U.N. plot to take over Sierra Leone.

Many believe that Sanko only continued talks with Bio through the election process to give RUF time to regroup from their losses to Executive Outcomes, resupply and rearm. In an intercepted radio communication between Sanko and his field commanders, Sanko stated that "he signed the accord only to relieve the military pressure and that he intended to purchase new arms and continue the war."[2] The rebels had renewed their practice of cutting off 'hands that could vote' and continued their attacks along the border where they still maintained control.

Meanwhile, back in Freetown, the elections were being led by Christian church leaders. Although Bio and his junta were allowing the election to go forward, they didn't actually want the elections to be held because Bio knew he would likely lose. So, the religious leaders of Sierra Leone joined together in a representative council and held a national conference in Freetown concerning the elections. They decided there would be a proportional representative government with candidates nominated by their people group.

In March 1996, Ahmed Kabbah, the leader of SLPP (Sierra Leone People's Party) was elected president by over 60 percent of the Sierra Leone population. Kabbah was openly Christian and elected as president of a country with a Muslim majority. He immediately set out to establish peace talks with the badly defeated RUF.

After the successful elections, the church began a period of national fasting in preparation for the peace talks. They fasted for 30 days, then 40 days and even 90 days. Christians were asked to fast from midnight to 6 PM the next day. This way the fasts could be carried on for an extended period.

While the church was fasting, newly elected President Kabbah and Foday Sanko were talking in Abidjan, the capital of Ivory Coast. Throughout the talks, RUF demanded that all peacekeeping forces, including the successful EO, leave Sierra Leone and they flatly rejected the outcome of the March 1996 election. The EO continued training the Kamajors as a suitable fighting force. They had already won several critical battles and brought RUF to the brink of defeat. Sanko was forced to concede on most of his demands, including the one that he be made a vice president, and that several top government positions be given to RUF leaders. Finally, on November 30, 1996, the Abidjan Peace Accords were signed.

The most critical outcomes of those peace accords were that all RUF soldiers received amnesty, RUF would become a political party (The Revolutionary United Front Party - RUFP), they could run candidates in elections, and Foday Sanko would receive a government position.

However, one of the most devastating consequences was that Executive Outcomes had to leave Sierra Leone. The International Monetary Fund issued a directive that said Sierra Leone would receive no further aid without first removing the extremely successful EO. To some, EO was a shady mercenary outfit. However, they had protected Freetown from invasion, taken back the diamond mines for RUF and forced them into peace talks that effectively ended the war...almost.

Within days of EO leaving, war returned.

The West, whose promises failed Sierra Leone again and again, believed they knew best. In demanding EO to leave, they doomed Sierra Leone to another five years of civil war. Many of the rebels feared they would be forced to go before tribunals and be sentenced to prison or even death for their crimes against humanity. So, they refused to come out of the bush. Their distrust also fueled their resistance to the Abidjan Peace Accords as a whole.

Kabbah had to calm factions within SLA that complained that his government was spending too much money on the Civil Defense Forces like the Kamajors. Meanwhile, Sanko was caught buying weapons in Nigeria and placed under house arrest. While SLA hesitated to act, Sanko put Sam Bockarie (known as Mosquito) in charge and RUF came roaring back.

Sam earned his nickname by his uncanny ability to attack his enemies when they were off-guard, particularly at night. He was also one of the most feared RUF leaders, well known for rape, mutilation, torture, and murder. He was made second-in-command of RUF by Taylor's NPFL Central Revolutionary Council allegedly because his sadistic nature and atrocities created so much panic and fear among the people.

As Mosquito began his reign of terror as leader of RUF, Foday

Sanko was hauled back to Freetown and sentenced to death. This should have been the end for Sanko. Instead, it was just the beginning of the church's role in reaching true peace with the rebels.

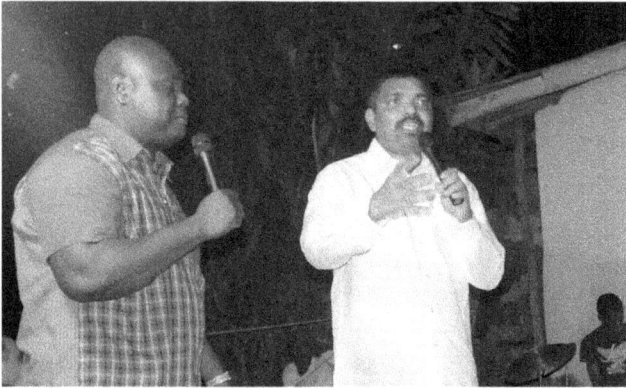

Brother Bennie preaching outside of Freetown, Sierra Leone with Dr. Patrick George.

Christian Osborn and Doc. Patrick at I-Don't-Care Crusade.

Steve with Dr. Sidikie and Sunil Church, on the way to inaugurating a new school in Sierra Leone.

Pastor Mathews Cherian with Pastor Kartik, Pastor Pitts, Siddiki and others at the Gethsemane Evangelical Mission headquarters in Freetown, Sierra Leone.

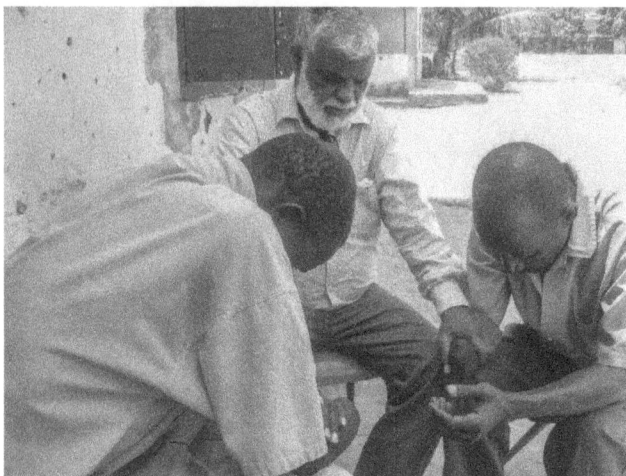

While visiting Sierra Leone, Pastor Mathews had the privilege to minister at various meetings throughout the country.

Pastor Mathews was moved by the stories of war. He personally was able to exhort, encourage, and pray with many amputees during his visit to West Africa.

7

THE ROAD LESS TAKEN

*It is the politicians who muddied the water
and it was the Christians who came along to
make sure that the water is crystal clear...*

REVEREND MOSES KHANU

I left Freetown to preach in Kono, one of the biggest mining districts in Sierra Leone. Kono is in the eastern part of Sierra Leone. The population is a mix of Christians, Muslims and many of the ethnic tribes. Countless people had lost their lives to the rebels and diamond mines in Kono. Over 120,000 people were killed and two million were displaced during Sierra Leone's civil war. Kono was left devastated by the war and needed to hear the gospel.

The farther from Freetown, the more pervasive the poverty. Fifty percent of the Freetown population is illiterate and in Kono, the number rises to 80 percent. In 2006, approximately 90 percent of school-age children in the area were not in school. There is no healthcare, and this results in the needless death of one-in-five children and one-in-twenty-three pregnant women.

The infrastructure of Sierra Leone and its people still bear the scars of the war. The roads are generally terrible and most of the roads in rural areas are littered with holes from grenades and bomb blasts.

On the way to Kono our car started smoking and we had to pull over to let it cool down. Eventually, someone came along and put soap powder in the radiator. I thought we were really in trouble, but it seemed to work, and we were able to keep traveling towards the border.

The night was pitch black as we tried to drive on what no one would ever call a road. The roads to Kono had knee-deep holes and divots meant to slow the army down when they entered the region. Between the dark night and a vehicle that overheated every few miles, it was one of the scariest drives of my life. The road was more of a suggestion; a possible way to go in the same sense that any space between two trees big enough for a car might be another possible way. We passed a check point and the guards warned us not to drive after dark. They said it was dangerous and we had to find a place to stay for the night. It wasn't too long after this that the radiator started smoking again. This time it happened right in front of a little village. Our driver got out to track down some of the miraculous radiator-healing soap powder, but the villagers thought we were thieves and there to rob them. I was getting a little nervous, but our driver was able to explain that we were preachers and our car was having problems. Eventually, we got on our way again and reached Kono.

I awoke the next morning to the sound of heavy rain, which made the roads even worse. Miles of wet clay and potholes stretched into the distance, but we finally reached the village where we were to preach. We walked up to the top of the mountain and found roughly 5,000 Sierra Leoneans gathered there, waiting to hear the gospel. The people of Kono had suffered for years under the attacks of RUF and SLA. Their broken government had continually let them down and the world had abandoned them. NGOs came with good intentions and grand promises but left after frustrations with the inability to overcome expensive and complex logistics, corruption and bureaucratic nightmares.

These 5,000 Kono villagers were hungry for something real: a hope that would never abandon them. They needed a promise that would remain true even in the face of poverty, disease, and death. They had a hunger and thirst for God.

———

After the 1996 election of President Kabbah, Christians in Sierra Leone were still making strides to bring national peace. The core group of church leaders who had led the 1996 elections officially formed IRCSL, the Inter-Religious Council of Sierra Leone. Reverend Khanu, President of the Council of Churches and the Evangelical Fellowship of Sierra Leone and the General Secretary of the Baptist Convention in Sierra Leone, helped establish IRCSL in 1997. They had clear goals of equipping and mobilizing cooperative efforts among the religious communities in Sierra Leone while taking concrete steps to restore stability and establish reconciliation and renewal in Sierra Leone. Reverend Khanu later said, "The Christian leaders played a very significant role compared to the politicians. This is so because if one has to be really realistic, it is the politicians who muddied the water and it was the Christians who came along to make sure that the water is crystal clear...If it were not for those organizations, I wonder what would have happened because the politicians see themselves as being chased by the rebels. Christians had confidence..."[1]

Due to the nature of religious tolerance in Sierra Leone, IRCSL was composed of Christian and Muslim organizations. The Christian members were the Council of Churches in Sierra Leone which represented 18 Protestant denominations, three Roman Catholic dioceses in (the Archdiocese of Freetown and Bo and the

Dioceses of Kenema and Makeni) and the Pentecostal Churches Council. The leaders of many of these religious groups had been active in the Abidjan peace talks in 1996 and saw the formation of the new umbrella group as the natural institutional continuation of their cooperation in using religious influence to facilitate a peaceful resolution of the conflict.

As IRCSL worked tirelessly to meet with the rebels and secure peace, they were often overlooked or completely ignored by the media. Their efforts were designated as "third-sector efforts" with the idea that if the military and the government could not secure peace, what chance did a bunch of pastors or priests have? Yet, with little support and few resources, they refused to give up.

IRCSL held a one-day multi-religious national conference in Freetown on April 1, 1997. Two hundred Muslim and Christian delegates from the areas of Sierra Leone that were not occupied by the rebels attended the conference. This officially launched IRCSL and their coordinated efforts to bring peace to Sierra Leone.

This document was called the Statement of Shared Moral Concerns. In part, it read,

> *"The people of Sierra Leone have undergone enormous suffering. But, thanks be to God, the peace accords have been signed. Our task now is to establish a durable peace based on truth, justice and common living and to collaborate with all people of good will in the healing tasks of reconciliation, reconstruction and rehabilitation for Sierra Leone. We, the responsible representatives of the Christian Churches and the Islamic Community in Sierra Leone recognize that our Religious Communities differ from each other and that each of them feels called to live true to its own faith. At the same time, we recognize that our religious and spiritual traditions hold many values in common and that these shared values can provide an authentic basis*

*for mutual esteem, cooperation and free common
living in Sierra Leone.*

*Each of our religious communities recognizes
that human dignity and human value is a gift of
God. Our religions, each in its own way, call us to
recognize the fundamental human rights of each
person. Violence against persons or the violation
of their basic rights are for us not only against
manmade laws but also break God's law.*

*We jointly, in mutual respectful recognition
of our religious differences, condemn all violence
against innocent persona and any form of abuse
or violation of fundamental human rights.*[2]

With the Abidjan Peace Accords quickly failing and RUF
surging again in the border areas of Sierra Leone under the
leadership of Sam "Mosquito" Bockarie, IRCSL met with President
Kabbah on May 23, 1997. They reminded Kabbah of the quickly
deteriorating situation and asked him to use them prominently in
the pursuit of peace. But only two days later, Kabbah was ousted
from office. The frustrations of SLA had reached the tipping point.
Continually frustrated by being wedged and marginalized between
RUF and the pro-Kabbah Kamajors and other Civil Defense Forces,
elements of SLA forged a coup.

A small group of SLA officers broke out 600 inmates from
Pademba Road Prison and armed them. They dragged out a former
SLA officer, Major Johnny Paul Koroma, put a gun to his head
and made him an offer he couldn't refuse: be president of Sierra
Leone or be shot. Johnny Paul had been a well-regarded soldier and
SLA leader, but in August 1996 he was arrested under suspicion
of preparing a coup against President Kabbah. He had been
languishing in Pademba Road Prison which was built to hold about
300 prisoners but now housed over 1,000. Johnny Paul had been
packed into an 8 by 10 foot cell with up to 30 other men and forced
to share a single bucket for a toilet.

Freed from prison but now facing certain death, Johnny Paul did what most reasonable men would do in that situation. He accepted the role of leader and asked the officers to kindly lower their guns. Johnny Paul and SLA immediately established AFRC, the Armed Forces Revolutionary Council.

In response, IRCSL condemned SLA's actions on international radio broadcasting stations and demanded Kabbah be returned to power. IRCSL leaders were already in a position where the country was looking to them for deliverance from the civil war. Their bold action during the coup continued to cement their critical role in the peace process.

Not surprisingly, IRCSL's demands were ignored by AFRC. Later, AFRC invited IRCSL to take part in the new government's inaugural ceremony of Johnny Paul, but IRCSL declined to participate. IRCSL continued to pursue dialogue with the military coup leaders and listened to their complaints while at the same time expressing condemnation of the coup and human rights abuses committed by Johnny Paul's junta. They tried hard to convince AFRC leaders to listen to the Sierra Leoneans and the international community and return the country to free elections and civilian rule. They also tried to convince them of the resolve of the people to engage in civil disobedience until free elections were held as well as the commitment of the international community to isolate the new regime. While IRCSL was unsuccessful in its efforts to persuade the junta to voluntarily return the country to civilian rule, many credit it with preventing even worse conditions when all other institutions in Sierra Leone had either collapsed or fled.

Sanko got wind of the coup while he was still under arrest in Nigeria. He knew he had an opportunity to exploit the chaos and confusion in the aftermath of the coup. He contacted Mosquito and ordered RUF forces to join in. Five thousand RUF rebels, angry and armed to the teeth, soon emerged from the bush and started a relentless march towards Freetown. When they reached the city, SLA barely fired a bullet. Instead, they greeted the rebels and proceeded to march through Freetown as comrades, side by side. AFRC leadership declared RUF leader, Foday Sanko, Deputy Chairman and the joint AFRC and RUF declared the war won and over.

It was not.

This road trip to Kono was an unbelievable experience.
The road was all dirt and we made the way as we traveled.

To Kono Village. "If you have men who will only come if they know there is a good road, I don't want them. I want men who will come if there is no road at all." —David Livingstone

Brother Bennie preaching at the Kono Crusade.

Brother Bennie with the Chief of Kono Village.

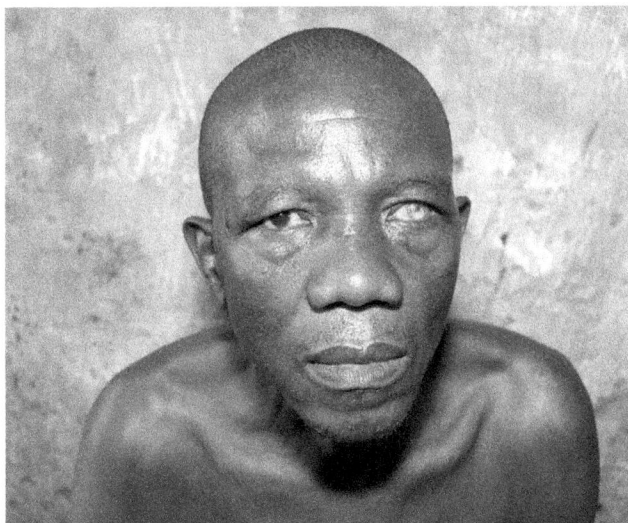

Former Civil War fighter.

A schoolteacher in Freetown.

8

OPERATION NO LIVING THING

It was the day of hell on earth.

SIERRA LEONE PASTOR,
speaking of January 6, 1999 now memorialized as J6.

Well, I am not God. But there is also no God to judge me.

A REBEL LEADER

From Nigeria, Sanko told both SLA and RUF to "take their reward." He said they had fought long and hard for many years and now they would receive their pay. It was time for "Operation Pay Yourself."

Five thousand RUF rebels joined with SLA's "Sobels". The rebels were already accustomed to raping, looting and murdering without fear of punishment. SLA soldiers were disillusioned, angry and wanted what they believed was due to them. Johnny Paul (some say by force) got on the radio and declared he had no money to pay them so the soldiers should loot and get whatever they wanted. Food was already in short supply. There was no electricity and the economy had completely collapsed. The citizens of Freetown were terrified. War had finally reached the capital city just when there should have been peace.

Paul Frank, a former Muslim who converted to Christianity, was living in Freetown when *Operation Pay Yourself* commenced in May 1997. He fearlessly ministered to churches in northern Sierra Leone throughout the war, but when *Operation Pay Yourself* began, he was trapped in Freetown. He zig-zagged through narrow back alleys as he tried to evade the rebels. He found an empty mission home and hid for as long as he could. Meanwhile, the rebels burned his house to the ground. Paul witnessed the rape and murder of many of his friends and neighbors. RUF and SLA soldiers strapped the bodies of their victims to the hoods of cars and drove them through the city to terrify anyone who survived. They cut various body parts off prisoners in public and then posted the pieces at intersections. The warning was, "Come join us now before we come to you."

Dr. Sidikie, the Freetown pastor who took me to different villages to preach, was hiding in his house with his wife and baby son, Isaac, during Operation Pay Yourself. The rebels had camped out on his front porch. They turned it into an overnight checkpoint where they would sleep for the night and move on in the morning. Apparently, they thought the house was empty and never tried to get inside. If they had known Dr. Sidikie and his family were inside, they would have either burned them alive in the house or kicked the door in, raped his wife and killed or at the very least, mutilated all three of them.

In the darkness and stifling heat, Dr. Sidikie and his wife tried not to make a sound. Then, Isaac began to cry. Terrified the rebels would hear his crying son and kill them all, Dr. Sidikie gathered his courage and did the unthinkable. He opened his front door and casually walked outside, acting like the rebels were his best friends. He complimented them and said he supported their cause.

He gave them a few dollars and told them to buy some bread and tea as his gift to them. Though he was trembling on the inside, the rebels thanked Dr. Sidikie and told him they would guard him for the night. Dr. Sidikie went back inside, closed the door and hugged his family.

The next morning, the soldiers were gone. God had saved their lives.

In the later days of *Operation Pay Yourself*, Dr. Sidikie was driving through Freetown with his son and had to pass Aberdeen Bridge. There was a general stationed at the bridge who called himself Evil Spirit. He killed anyone he wanted to and would have their bodies thrown over the bridge into the water below. But there was no way for him to turn around without attracting attention.

When Dr. Sidikie pulled up to the checkpoint, he realized his son didn't have his papers, ensuring he would be accused of being a rebel. The checkpoint soldier outside the building asked Dr. Sidikie for their papers. Dr. Sidikie handed him his papers but had nothing to give him for his son. The soldier looked up and into the checkpoint house where General Evil Spirit waited. Dr. Sidikie silently prayed for his son's life. The soldier looked back down at the papers and leaned inside the car. Quietly, he said, "Go, quickly. If the General sees you, he will kill you!" Dr. Sidikie drove away and his son's life was saved.

Dr. Patrick George was confronted by the rebels in Freetown during this time as well. He made a statement in public that was deemed negative towards SLA. He was caught and thrown into a shipping container for two days and later released by ECOMOG troops.

Though it seems impossible that Johnny Paul was a Christian, every pastor I spoke with in Sierra Leone was convinced he was a Christian who was forced to be a leader and give commands at gunpoint. James Farmer, the fearless Gideon International worker who took Bibles to the rebels in the bush, told me of the day Johnny Paul called upon him to pray with him. A car pulled up and James was ordered to get inside. He was driven to AFRC headquarters.

Johnny Paul was in a meeting, so James sat and waited for two hours. During that time, he began praying with the soldiers and officials waiting in the room with him. One man he spoke with accepted Christ right there in the headquarters lobby. Eventually, James was called in to meet Johnny Paul. There, he fearlessly shared the gospel with the entire room and prayed with Johnny Paul.

The western world did not have a high opinion of Johnny Paul or his AFRC party. The U.N. condemned the coup and isolated Sierra Leone by establishing a naval and road blockade. Foreign governments withdrew their diplomats. ECOMOG said they would withdraw their forces unless Kabbah was reinstated. This was that threat which caused AFRC and RUF to enter into new negotiations in 1997. In October of that year, they agreed to the Conakry Peace Plan, but just like every other peace plan, it quickly fell apart with no results.

Right after the Conakry Peace Plan was established, ECOMOG retook Freetown and reinstated Kabbah as president. But in a critical mistake, ECOMOG didn't completely defeat the fleeing rebel forces or even drive them very far from Freetown. The rebels holed up right outside Freetown and waited for the opportunity to strike back at ECOMOG. They did not have to wait very long.

━━━━━━━━━━━━━━━━━

January 6, 1999 is a date known to every single Freetown Sierra Leonean. They may not remember the exact date they had their arm or foot chopped off or watched their family members killed. But they remember January 6, 1999. As one pastor told me, it was the day of "hell on earth."

AFRC/RUF forces were intent on retaking Freetown. They named their plan 'Operation No Living Thing'. It was also called Annihilate Every Living Thing. The goal was to make all the destruction and terror they had unleashed on Sierra Leone in the previous year pale in comparison.

RUF rebels snuck into Freetown to start the invasion. They

dismantled guns and hid them under bundles of leaves. That way they could later return as if they were only coming to sell vegetables in the market.

The news came early in the morning at 2 AM. The radio station 98.1, the only source of critical news on the war for the citizens of Freetown, broadcast the news that the rebels were in Waterloo and on their way. The rebels who had already snuck into Freetown were armed and waiting. They had closed the only two remaining entry and exit points of the city, the highway to Waterloo and the sea. Freetown was trapped.

Arunabah was a Christian truck driver who had driven to Freetown from Bo to pick up some goods at the harbor. He was supposed to be in and out of Freetown on the 5th of January.
But the goods were delayed a day, so he stayed overnight in a small house with 14 other people.

The rebels surrounded the house and called all of them outside. They made them stand in a line and demanded they tell them the location of ECOMOG troops. No one knew, certainly not Arunabah. The rebels went down the line killing each person one by one demanding the location of the ECOMOG troops. Suddenly, Arunabah was the only one left standing. This was a common tactic of the rebels. Leave only one person alive. The purpose was so that man, woman or child could tell others how terrifying the rebels were and create a sense of helplessness among the citizens.

When the head rebel stood directly in front of Arunabah and looked into his eyes, Arunabah realized he knew him! He had helped him before the war. He begged him, since he showed him goodness in the past, to let him live. The rebel thought about it.

"Well, I am not God. But there is also no God to judge me. So, I will let you live, but I will take one of your arms." Arunabah was pushed to the ground and pinned by the soldiers. It took two blows to take his right arm.

Paul Frank, who had barely escaped from his burning house in *Operation Pay Yourself,* holed up once again in the abandoned mission house. He hid in a small underground hole. At night, the rebel soldiers stood on the unfinished columns of the house and fired at ECOMOG soldiers, right above him, the whole time. He had to stay in that hole for over a week until he had a chance to safely get out and find safety.

Raymond Lavaly was a Methodist preacher in the Kambia district during the war. Too many times he had fled from village to village as each one was invaded and burned down. He and his family had been safe in Kambia for a while, but eventually, the rebels attacked there as well. Kambia is close to the coast and Raymond, his family and other surviving villagers fled into a swampy area close to the sea. Most of them could not swim and drowned. Raymond also couldn't swim and was carried by his fellow villagers until they were hit by bullets. Raymond went down into the swampy water, struggled up three times and then sank helplessly to the bottom. As he lost consciousness, he felt an arm grab him and pull him to the surface before dragging him to shore. He and his family survived the attack.

Raymond moved his family to Freetown thinking it was safer, but just 2 months later, he was back in the crosshairs of the rebels during *Operation No Living Thing*. His wife had gone to the market just before the operation commenced. He was home alone with his 6-year-old daughter. He looked outside his window as his neighbor friend ran from his house and was shot in the shoulder. Raymond ran outside, used his own shirt to try to stop the bleeding and dragged him into his house. He had just managed to hide him in his attic when rebels broke down his front door and demanded he come outside. To go outside meant death so Raymond decided he would rather die in his house with his young daughter, protecting his friend.

Strangely, when Raymond refused to exit, the rebels didn't shoot him. They asked him if he smoked or drank. When Raymond answered that he did not, they told him to get them cigarettes and alcohol or they would kill him and his daughter. The rebels watched Raymond as he walked outside and began knocking on doors. But no one would answer him or open their door. The rebels told him they would go around back and make sure no one from inside tried to run out the back. Raymond saw his opportunity. With the rebels momentarily out of sight he ran back to his house, grabbed his daughter and ran down the street. He saw a small house that looked empty and burst inside before shutting the door behind him. He looked up and saw a small storage space in the ceiling. He pulled himself and his daughter up into the space and tried to catch his breath. Outside, he could hear the rebels yelling as they searched for him. Their shouts grew closer and louder until they were at the front door. They tried to kick it in, but the door held. Bullets tore through the walls. After the gunfire stopped, Raymond realized both he and his daughter were still alive and unharmed. Then he smelled smoke. The rebels had set the house on fire. Raymond prayed out to God for deliverance. Then he realized the rebels had moved on, certain that they had shot him or that he would soon burn to death. The fire didn't spread, and the flames died out in minutes. Raymond and his daughter waited in the crawl space until night and fled to the countryside under the cover of darkness.

An estimated 7,000 people were killed during *Operation No Living Thing*. Over half of those dead were civilians.

James, a Gideon Bible deliverer.

Dr. Patrick George and Dr. Sidikie.

Brother Bennie visiting the construction site of a new school building, with the leadership team in Sierra Leone.

9

BULLETS INTO CROSSES

Even in this dark moment of our nation, Lord, I ask this nation to join me to proclaim the Lord Jesus Christ as our Lord and Savior and to proclaim you Heavenly Father as the ruler of this nation. We shall overcome. We shall overcome in the name of Jesus.

JOHNNY PAUL KOROMA,
National Prayer, 1997

I laughed a little in the mayor's office in Freetown. I was finally able to meet with him the day I was scheduled to leave. I was so excited to tell him I had not forgotten him or the people of Sierra Leone...but he didn't remember me.

I jogged his memory a little about our previous meeting and conversation on the plane and how he invited me to his country. Still, he didn't remember me. Again, I laughed because it confirmed that God did not bring me to Sierra Leone to be friends with the president or the mayor. That did not matter. It was not the most important thing. God used the mayor, just as He used Courage, to bring me to Sierra Leone so that His gospel would be shared, souls would be declared His and further work established where it was needed.

In fact, the day before, we had a special prayer meeting with the President of Sierra Leone, Earnest Bai Koroma. President Koroma was the fourth president of Sierra Leone and served from 2007 to 2018. He was also a Christian and regularly invited pastors to come and pray with him at the beginning of each week. I was invited to be a part of that meeting and was speechless at how the Lord had orchestrated all these things. I could not wait to share these amazing stories with Lina and my parents. I was keenly aware that so many of these events were also the answer to my parents' prayers.

To meet the mayor of Freetown again was a great reconnection and as we were leaving his office, I asked him if I could pray for him. He said he would love that and asked that I pray for his flight to America that evening. Turns out, we were to be on the very same BMI Airlines flight via London. Pastor Henry joked, "There you go again, flying together."

I was advised to go to the airport early specifically because I was Indian. Since so many Indians own and work in the diamond mines, they had to go through additional levels of security at the airport. Sure enough, I was delayed and had to go through extra screening and answer many questions. When my turn came, the officer looked at me very seriously and instructed me to open my luggage. I had two bags because we take things for people when making mission trips which means we sometimes return with an empty bag. Suspicious, the security officer started questioning me and I knew it was going to be a long and annoying wait. Just then, I heard an entourage of people heading into the airport behind me. I turned around to look and it was the Mayor with his security personnel. I yelled, "Hello, Mayor Williams!" He came over and greeted me, "Mathews, we will see you later."

The mayor greeted me, and I said hello back. The guard noticed. The security officer looked on in surprise.

"You know him? The mayor?" the guard asked.

"Yes." I replied.

"So, you are on a state visit?"

"No, something bigger than that." I replied, "I am a servant of the Most High God. I am here for the King of Kings and the Lord of Lords."

"You are a man of God?" He asked intently.

"Yes"

"You can go."

If I had turned down Pastor Henry's invitation to Sierra Leone, I would have missed so many divinely orchestrated opportunities. Seeing souls saved. Seeing what the Lord was doing in a war-torn country for His glory. Connecting with the Lord's appointment of a believing mayor and president.

With that, I gathered my things and boarded my flight with all I had witnessed and experienced weighing heavily on my heart.

———

In an incredible opportunity after *Operation No Living Thing*, Ugandan diplomat Francis Okelo, then serving in Sierra Leone as the special envoy of the UN secretary-general, invited IRCSL to try to open a dialogue between the re-instated President Kabbah and RUF leader Foday Sanko. Sanko was a prisoner of the government at the time. The politicians looked to the Church to bring the peace they could not. Reverend Khanu took the lead.

Right before *Operation No Living Thing*, Foday had been moved from Pademba Road Prison to the hull of a ship offshore. The last victory the rebels needed was to free their leader. Now that it was over, Reverend Khanu and other pastors took Foday and drove him around Freetown to see the death and destruction his soldiers had waged during *Operation No Living Thing*. Here were Christian men fearlessly forcing one of the most feared and brutal men in all of Africa to confront the evil and destruction he had caused in the name of a revolution "for the people".

After the tour, they took Foday into a building where they could sit and talk to him. Reverend Khanu sat right next to him. At first, Foday was prideful and arrogant. He ranted for 45 minutes about why he was waging war and tried to justify his actions. The pastors sat and listened. Finally, one woman interrupted him. She stood up with tears in her eyes and pleaded with him, on behalf of all the women in Sierra Leone, to please stop the horrific acts his men were carrying out. With that, Foday sank down in his chair. His arrogance gone. He knew he had no defense. IRCSL told him they wanted a solution. Foday said he hadn't been in touch with RUF for three years. But he would be willing to talk to its leadership. He also wanted to talk to the U.N.

Reverend Khanu and the rest of IRCSL met with President Kabbah and told him to allow Foday to talk to Mosquito, Foday's second-in-command. Kabbah agreed. Foday spoke with Mosquito over ham radio and called for a cease-fire later that day.

After that, IRCSL began to meet with Foday on a weekly basis. They would take him from the ship's hull to special meeting facilities. The locations would change each time for security reasons and at one point, they met at military barracks to ensure there were no escape attempts or attacks from the rebels. With each visit, these men and women were putting their lives at risk. Foday was both a high-risk target and a valuable asset to free at any cost.

Rebels higher up in RUF contacted IRCSL leadership and said they wanted to meet with them out in the bush. They had taken children during Operation No Living Thing and offered to release them if IRCSL met with them. Reverend Khanu was apprehensive at first. To meet in the bush with the rebels meant they could easily be killed. The meeting place was beyond the last ECOMOG security checkpoint. Once they crossed that, they were completely at the mercy of the rebels. But Khanu also knew this was an opportunity to bring the peace for which they had so fervently fasted and prayed. IRCSL prayed and then agreed to meet.

When Rev. Khanu and IRCSL arrived at the agreed upon meeting location outside Waterloo, they could see the rebels in the distance. The rebels had the child hostages in front of them and had tied white ribbons around their heads and wrists.

First, IRCSL handed over 20 bags of rice and two bags of sugar, each weighing 50 kilos, which were donated by the government. In return, RUF released 23 hostages; 20 of them being children ranging in age from five to 17 years old. With the initial promises kept, the peace talk commenced.

They sat on benches in a small circle. The rebels surprised IRCSL by asking to pray. Their prayer wound up a mix of Christianity and Islam, a reflection of the syncretic religion practiced in the RUF camps. When Rev Khanu opened his eyes and looked up, he saw hidden RUF soldiers slowly emerging from the bush. They had been hiding to form an ambush in case anything went wrong. The ECOMOG soldier who had accompanied IRCSL was disarmed. The moment was tense. But once the soldier was disarmed, the rebels relaxed.

Rev. Khanu remembers that the rebels had a very loud sheep. It was walking around them and bleating. They said they had caught it as a lamb. One of the rebels had enough and told the sheep to be quiet and instantly it laid down and was quiet for the rest of the two-hour meeting.

They drank tea and talked about peace. The members of IRCSL could tell the rebels were weary and ready to lay down their arms under the right conditions. Peace was within their grasp.

After the meeting, one of the rebels took money and gave it to the only woman member of IRCSL who had attended.

IRCSL returned to Freetown and spoke with President Kabbah. By this time, Kabbah was worn down from the fighting, the coup attempt, the siege of Freetown and the weakening support of the Nigerians in ECOMOG. He wanted peace as much as RUF did and he was willing to make sacrifices.

IRCSL worked to set up an official and neutral venue for peace talks. First, they considered Norway, but Foday refused to go. They held consultations with traditional chieftains, members of parliament, representatives of civil society groups and Liberian President Charles Taylor, who was still RUF's main backer. Afterwards, RCSL again met separately with Kabbah and Sanko and convinced them that the only hope for successful negotiations would be a neutral venue. Over the objections of his cabinet, Kabbah released Sanko and allowed him to travel to Lomé in Togo where President Gnassingbé Eyadéma held the rotating Economic Community of West African States (ECOWAS) chairmanship.

Once in Togo, IRCSL members stayed in the same hotel as Foday and would even converse with the rebels in the restaurants and around the hotel grounds during breaks from the official peace talks. They would pray with some of them. When the talks would break down, they called the rebels to the restaurant and lobbied with them. They explained it was a negotiation. The rebels would agree to go back and keep working.

On May 18, 1999, a cease-fire between the government and the rebels was signed by Kabbah and Sanko. One week later, formal peace negotiations began which led to the July 7 signing of the Lomé Peace Agreement. IRCSL had succeeded in bringing together the head of state, rebel leaders and all participants in the conflict, in a dialogue that brought about the first real step in the peaceful resolution to the Sierra Leone Civil War.

On account of its outstanding mediation and results, international facilitating groups and the sides in the conflict granted IRCSL "Track One" status in peace negotiations. This was an incredible testament to the key role IRCSL played in the negotiation process. Track One is an official designation and "usually considered to be the primary peacemaking tool of a state's foreign policy. It is carried out by diplomats, high-ranking government officials and heads of states and is aimed at influencing the structures of political power."[1]

One of IRCSL's first initiatives after the Lomé Peace Agreement was to establish Disarmament, Demobilization and Reintegration camps or DDRs. The camps were set up across Sierra Leone and offered rebel soldiers clothes, food and shelter in return for their weapons. The rebels had to agree to stay in the camp for a six-week period during which they would learn vocational skills that would help them become productive members of society.

Overall, the DDR camps were successful. It is estimated that by 2002, 45,000 weapons had been confiscated and 70,000 rebel soldiers had been processed.[2] Jeff, a Kamajor fighter-turned-Christian, entered a DDR camp in 2002 after hearing the message from the government that it was time for reconciliation. Now was the time to come out of the bush, forgive and heal.

"Can you imagine being in the bush and coming out just because someone tells you to?" He told me. "That is only through God." Not long after, Jeff began attending church. He said it was like he finally came to his senses. He realized the horrible sinfulness of his actions. He not only became a Christian; he now serves as a pastor.

_____

In the midst of burgeoning peace, there was still certain RUF elements that refused to lay down arms. Although ECOMOG was gone, the United Nations Mission to Sierra Leone or UNAMSIL took its place. What started out as 6,000 troops grew to be 17,500 by March 2001. This was the largest UN force in history but it almost became another disaster.

UNAMSIL was deployed in the mining areas. Yet, it frequently lost battles to the rebels who refused to abide by the Peace Accords. In May 2000, over 500 UNAMSIL troops were captured and held hostage by RUF. The rebels took their weapons and vehicles. Mosquito, still holding out and in charge of RUF, headed towards Freetown for another attack. UNAMSIL grew wary of fighting battles they could lose and changed their strategy to one of avoidance, much as SLA troops had years earlier in the conflict. It was an embarrassment for the United Nations and the entire western involvement in the peace process. Even their largest force couldn't muster the will to defeat the few rebels left. Now, the Peace Accords were on the verge of collapse.

Although Kabbah was president at the time, Johnny Paul Koroma was SLA's Lieutenant Colonel even after being previously deposed by ECOMOG forces. While Kabbah's government could barely govern beyond Freetown, Johnny Paul had the very real power of, at least, 5,000 soldiers. When Johnny heard that the rebels were once again approaching Freetown, he immediately went on national radio 98.1. He told his soldiers to arm themselves and be prepared. He also declared that at 6 PM, every citizen of Freetown was to go out into the streets and shout the name of Jesus as loud as they could seven times. After a decade of bloody fighting, the devastation of an entire country and the official Peace Accords hanging by a thread, the leader of the Sierra Leone army called on Jesus to save Freetown from yet another horrific attack.

RUF rebels were just outside Freetown by late afternoon and closing in. Johnny Paul ran out into the street with a megaphone. "Jesus! Jesus! Jesus!" He yelled the Lord's name over and over. Dr. Sidikie and his wife, with little Isaac in their arms, rushed out into the streets and began shouting the name of Jesus. For Dr. Sidikie and his wife along with all the other Christians shouting the name of Jesus in the streets, it wasn't some meaningless name shouted in some sort of chant. Theirs was the ultimate prayer of desperation as they sought intervention from God. It was a prayer of pleading, salvation, hope, and rescue all rolled into one. They cried out to the God to whom they had fasted and prayed for so many days. Each shout was a remembrance of all the deaths, all the horrors and all the children killed or lost to RUF.

Idrissa, the boy soldier who escaped the rebels when they ordered him to burn down the school, was there as well. After he fled from ECOMOG soldiers indiscriminately killing civilians on the bridge and found the Bible, he hid in the jungle for a week. He had no food or water and survived by drinking malumbo, a liquid found in one of the jungle plants. Eventually, he made his way to a refugee camp on the outskirts of Freetown. Idrissa clearly remembers May 9th when he saw Johnny Paul in the streets with a megaphone in one hand and his gun in the other, shouting the name of Jesus. He could also see the approaching rebels, guns raised and ready. They had reached Freetown! They were right there, in the streets and marching towards Johnny Paul and the crowds of civilians. The shouts still filled the air as Idrissa waited for the sound of gunfire to erupt. But then in complete surprise, he watched as the rebels stopped and put their guns down on the ground. He couldn't believe his eyes. These rebels were the same men who took lives without blinking. But they had laid down their guns. Then they walked away. It was the last attack on Freetown.

Later that month, 1,200 British paratroopers were brought in through Operation Palliser. They reinforced the faltering UNAMSIL troops. RUF bases in Guinea were bombed and Liberia was pressured to expel all RUF soldiers and end financial support. The Kamajors ended their operations once they saw that RUF was dissolving.

On January 18, 2002, President Kabbah officially proclaimed the end of the Sierra Leone Civil War. It had lasted eleven long, terrible and violent years. Once again, it was time for free elections in Sierra Leone.

The churches coordinated a country-wide three-day fast. IRCSL took empty bullet casings and had them twisted into crosses and put on necklaces. They handed them out all over Freetown. In May 2002, the presidential election was held and Kabbah was re-elected as president while his party, Sierra Leone People's Party (SLPP), won a large majority in Parliament.

IRCSL continued to work hard. They developed strategic assistance for those in need. They took supplies into the jungle to begin the process of reintegration with the rebels whom they also offered counseling while reassuring them they could be forgiven. In 2003, IRCSL began community-based reconciliation through the Truth and Reconciliation Commission. The goal of the commission was to "create an impartial historical record of violations and abuses of human rights and international humanitarian law

related to the armed conflict in Sierra Leone, from the beginning
of the conflict in 1991 to the signing of the Lomè Peace Agreement;
to address impunity, to respond to the needs of the victims, to
promote healing and reconciliation and to prevent a repetition of
the violations and abuses suffered."[3] The Commission was initially
planned to last for nine months but continued for over a year.
IRCSL members worked in pairs to document the confessions of
rebel soldiers.

IRCSL provided counseling for countless number of women
who had been raped and abused. They brought them clothes and
cared for them. These women had been crippled by their experience
and the social stigma that followed. So, IRCSL gave them a new
identity and a much greater chance of being married, which is
essential in African culture. Many of the women were bush wives
who bore the children of the rebel soldiers who raped them. The
children had never received proper names until that time.

The Special Court for Sierra Leone was established in 2002 by
Sierra Leone and the United Nations in order to prosecute the worst
offenders of the war. The proceedings were slow but successful. For
many of the war criminals, their lives ended as violently, dismally or
mysteriously as they had been lived. Foday Sanko hopped a fence
and escaped from Freetown only to be captured again and placed
under house arrest. In 2000, his personal cadre of soldiers fired on
a group of protesters outside his home and killed 20 of them. Foday
was arrested, handed over to the British and indicted on 17 war-
crime counts. He suffered, at least, one stroke in jail and by the
time of his court appearances, he was still suffering the effects. At
his last public appearance in court, he said, "I am a god. I am a god
in the jungle." He died in prison on July 29, 2003, before his trial
was completed.

His second-in-command was not so lucky. Sam "Mosquito"
Bockarie fled Sierra Leone in 2000 to Liberia where he teamed

up with then Liberian President, Charles Taylor. But once he was back in Liberia, Taylor was scared he would testify against him at the Special Court. It is claimed Taylor told him to meet him on a beach. There, the Liberian president had Bockarie tortured and murdered. After Mosquito was tortured to death, his family, aides and bodyguard were summarily executed on President Taylor's orders. The official story is that he was killed in a shoot-out on May 5, 2003. Nothing about Bockarie and Taylor's action could ever be heard by the media or the Special Court.

Johnny Paul Koroma was a hero to the people of Sierra Leone, but his AFRC troops aligned with the rebels and committed human rights violations. For that, he was indicted by the Special Court. He fled the country and, reportedly, ended up in Liberia as well. Johnny Paul was declared dead on June 1, 2003. His death was as mysterious as his motives. Some say he met the same fate as Mosquito and was murdered by Taylor. Still, some newspapers reported that he was alive and had an army of 1,000 men.

Out of all of them, Charles Taylor was the biggest criminal. In 2012, he was convicted of 11 charges including terrorism, rape, murder and other inhumane acts. He was the first African head of state to be convicted by the Special Court of Sierra Leone. Charles was sentenced to 50 years in prison and is serving his sentence at HM Prison Frankland in North East England. He was 64 years old at his sentencing. He will die in prison.

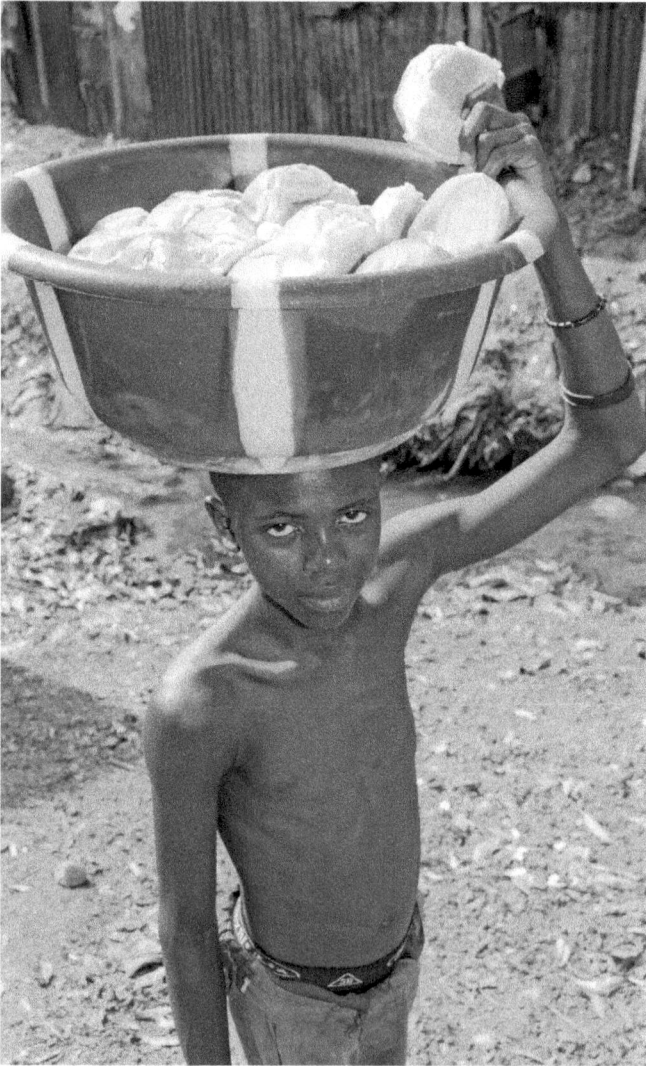

Child selling bread on the streets of Freetown.

*Brother Bennie, Sierra Leone's President Earnest Bhai Koroma,
Dr. Evans and a visiting delegation at the President's House.*

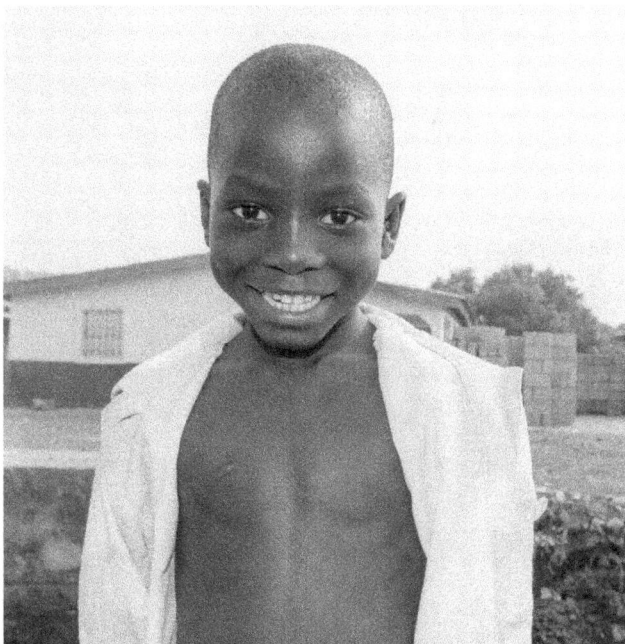

May the joy of the Lord be their strength.

Brother Bennie, preaching in a church outside of Freetown.

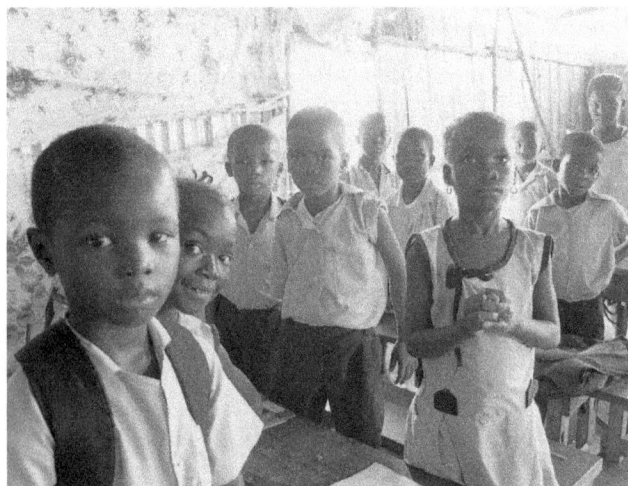

Schoolchildren of Sierra Leone.

10

THE BUTCHERS BECOME THE PEACEKEEPERS

Mourn with those who mourn

ROMANS 12:15

I traveled back to Sierra Leone in 2012 with my co-writer, Daniel. We went to the town of Waterloo to preach. It was the same village where I met the man who had been shot through the head and lived to tell the tale.

Before I was to preach, Daniel and I walked through the village. A lady called out to me. Her English was broken so I wasn't sure what she was saying, but she was surrounded by other women and children and they were all motioning for me to come over. She told me she was unable to have children. For a woman in Africa, where many children are not only expected but needed, barrenness is devastating. When she told me her condition, it touched my heart because my wife Lina and I were also unable to have children for so long. We prayed and put our trust in God and soon enough, He gave us three beautiful children. I asked the woman if she was a believer and she said she was. So, I laid my hand on her head and prayed over her, asking God to heal her and give her the blessing of many children.

Once again, I thought of the woman with the blood issue who reached out to Jesus, desperate for even the hem of His garment. She had spent all her money on doctors and had suffered for 12 long years. And then, she reached out to her only true hope, Jesus Christ.

Later that night, I awoke at 4 AM to the sounds of a woman wailing loudly outside. I was sleeping on the third floor of the mission house and she was walking through the slum area below, crying out an Islamic prayer over and over. The sound of desperation and mourning in this woman's voice crying out in the darkness and carrying through my window at four in the morning was enough to give me chills and fill my heart with sadness. I thought surely someone must have died, maybe her husband or child. But, there was nothing I could do.

Her lament reminded me of the cries in the Scripture. The rich man cried out from hell to Abraham up in Heaven and asked for him to send Lazarus with just a single drop of water, but his cries came too late. I never want to hear the cries that are too late. That is why we must reach out and reach the unreached now, while they might be found.

Reaching the unreached means reaching out as Jesus reached out: to the lame and the crippled. In Sierra Leone, this means reaching out to those who cannot reach back. They cannot take your hand because they have lost theirs.

Edward Conteh, the man who went to get water for his thirsty children and wound up losing his right arm, became president of the Sierra Leone Amputee and War-Wounded Association. He, with a staff of only four, tries to assist the needs of over

27,000 amputees.

I met with him in his office in Freetown. He is a man with a deep gravelly voice. He was hesitant to talk to me, not because of fear but from weariness. He was tired of talking. He had talked to everyone he possibly could. They all said they would help and then they all left. He was talked out and tired of believing.

"We need a Moses!" He exclaimed to me. "Many of the churches in the West were here during the war, but now they have gone. We need them back! The local churches care, but they cannot afford to do anything to truly help."

He showed me a bulletin board with various photos pinned to it. He tapped a photo of a boy who was missing both arms. "He was a toddler when the rebels took his arms. He is dead now. He recently died." I think about Edward often, troubled by his words of a Western church that never came back to help.

Sheku Conteh, the young man who left his arm on a riverbank, made it to an amputee camp by 2002. He lived there with his wife and children who had escaped the attack on their village. Although he survived, he received little assistance from the government. His only option is to beg for bowls of rice for his family to avoid starvation. Though he is a Christian, some days he wonders if it would have been better if he had been killed instead of being maimed.

Arunabah, the driver who lost his arm during Operation No Living Thing, made it to a French amputee camp operated by Médecins Sans Frontières (Doctors Without Borders). There, he received a prosthetic arm and is now driving his truck and earning a sustainable wage.

Most of the help amputees have received has come through NGO's and the church, but certainly not through the Sierra Leone government. They are understandably frustrated and feel deserted and exploited by Western journalists. Many in the amputee camps simply refused to talk with me or be photographed. They were tired of talking and seeing no results.

The wounded survivors are barely remembered, and the dead

are too easily forgotten. Over 50,000 lay dead by the end of the war with mass graves still being uncovered and secured by special forensic teams brought in by the Special Court and the Truth and Reconciliation Commission.

━━━━━━━━━━━━━━━━

The Civil War dramatically transformed the Christian church in Sierra Leone through exile, unity and awareness. The pastors who went into exile, spread Christianity within the refugee camps. They caused a major revival of Christianity in Guinea. When these pastors came back, they displayed a renewed dedication. They were filled with a rekindled vigor. Before the war, the church was dormant in many ways. Now, evangelism has become a priority and Christianity has spread across Sierra Leone.

Christians also facilitated a beautiful current wave of forgiveness. James, the Gideon Bible deliverer, told me, "That is how they are in this country. It is in the nature of Sierra Leoneans to forget. We do not hold on to grudges."

God grows His church through trials and though this war purpose was not persecution against Christians, it was the suffering of the saints amid their terrible trials which pushed them to their knees and caused them to cry out to God to save their lives. Sierra Leone was dedicated to God and the little country dominated by Muslims now has a strong Christian presence and a vibrant church.

In 2011, Sierra Leone sent peacekeeping troops to Darfur. A newspaper headline read, *The Butchers Become the Peacekeepers.* All of us, as sinners, were once wicked and evil just like so many fighters in Sierra Leone's civil war. We were separated from God and our sins caused Christ to be butchered on the cross. Yet, through the redeeming work of the cross, we can be at peace with God and become peacemakers by preaching the gospel to all mankind and bring other folks to peace with God.

IRCSL is still alive and active in Sierra Leone. There are still country-wide fasts and days of prayer. I ask you, when was the last time our great "Christian" nation of America had a national day of fasting and prayer? In Sierra Leone, they know they are weak and need God's provision and care. They also need the help of the Western church and NGOs. There is still Edward, struggling everyday with the burden of carrying for a country of war-scarred amputees.

Most recently, there is a new killer, Ebola. It emerges from the jungle and kills as terribly and painfully as the rebels once did. The Ebola outbreak from 2013-2016 brought a new terror to Sierra Leone and over 11,000 deaths in Western Africa, with Sierra Leone being the most affected.

I was so grateful to the Lord that my father, Pastor Cherian Mathews was able to travel to Sierra Leone and visit with those that had lived through the horrific war. Always an encourager, he met with amputees and would keep the people of Sierra Leone on his heart. In 2016 when the Ebola epidemic was threatening, he prayed for the country and Christian leaders via a video message. God answered his prayer.

What can we do for Sierra Leone? First and foremost, pray for Sierra Leone. Second, get involved. Learn about missions and Christian NGOs helping in Sierra Leone. See if they need help. Give financially or take a trip and serve in Sierra Leone for a season. Third, raise awareness. Use social media and other means to urge others to learn about Sierra Leone—their needs and how to help.

When the world discovered the deaths of six million Jews at the end of World War II, they built memorials and said, "Never again". When the world discovered the bodies of one million butchered Rwandan Hutus, they built memorials and said, "Never again". When the world saw the mass graves in Bosnia, they built memorials and said, "Never again". But as Christians we know better. Evil acts will happen again. When it does, we cannot turn away. We cannot pretend these are not our brothers and sisters. These are members of our body. We must look and understand even if it horrifies us. We must act.

God alone can end atrocities like the Sierra Leone Civil War, and He chooses to do so through His church. If a person, or country, touches the hem of His garment, they will be healed. Sierra Leone desperately reached for God and experienced His healing and forgiveness.

Pray for the church in Sierra Leone.

National Office for the Amputee and War Wounded Association, Freetown.

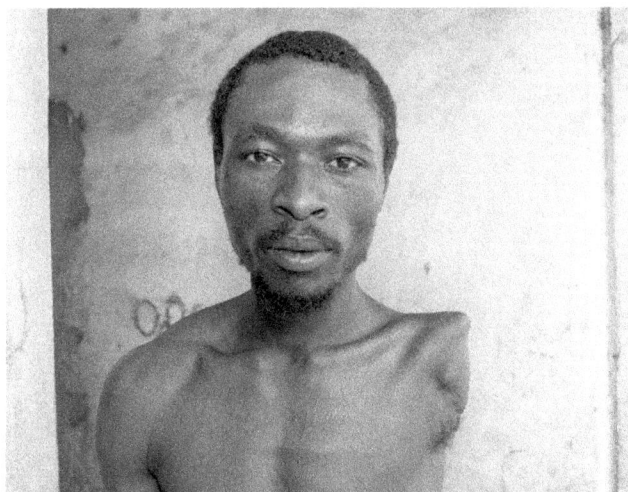

Civil War amputee.

Amputee survivor, Edward Conteh.

The face of innocence. Pray for a future for her in Christ.

GLOSSARY

AFRC - *The Armed Forces Revolutionary Council.*
Established by Johnny Paul Koroma in 1997.

ECOMOG - *The Economic Community Cease Fire Monitoring Group*

ECOWAS - *The Economic Community of West African States*

IRCSL - *Inter-Religious Council of Sierra Leone.*
Headed by Reverend Khanu.

Kamajors - *Cult-like warriors from the Mende tribe*

NPFL - *The National Patriotic Front of Liberia   RUF - Revolutionary*
United Front. Led by Foday Sanko.

RUFP - *Revolutionary United Front Party.*

SLA - *Sierra Leone Army*

TRC - *Truth and Reconciliation Committee*

UNAMSIL - *United Nations Mission in Sierra Leone*

UNHCR - *United Nations High Commissioner for Refugees*

ENDNOTES

Chapter 2
1. Moody, D. (2016). *North-Western Hymn Book*. Forgotten Books.
2. Abraham, A. (1987). *The Amistad Revolt: A Historical Legacy of Sierra Leone and the United States*. [ebook] United States Information Service. Available at: http://www.sierraleone.org/Books/Amistad.pdf.
3. Ibid.
4. Bowen, J. (1862). *Memorials of John Bowen, Late Bishop of Sierra Leone*. London: J. Nisbet, p.554.
5. "Key Players Overview". Sierra Leone Ministry of Mineral Resources. 21 January 2010. Retrieved 19 March 2011.
6. Kimberleyprocess.com. (2019). *Sierra Leone | Kimberley Process*. [online] Available at: https://www.kimberleyprocess.com/en/sierra-leone-0.
7. Campbell, G. (2012). *Blood Diamonds, Revised Edition*. New York: Basic Books, p.10.
8. Brilliant Earth. (2018rr). *Brilliant Earth*. [online] Available at: https://www.brilliantearth.com/conflict-diamond-child-labor/ [Accessed 17 Mar. 2018].
9. Sachs, J.D. & Warner, A.M. (1995). *"Natural Resource Abundance and Economic Growth"*. NBER Working Paper (5398). This concept is not new. Observations go back hundreds of years, but this was one of the first studies, and most influential, to demonstrate a correlation.
10. Hdr.undp.org. (2018). *Human Development Reports*. [online] Available at: http:// hdr.undp.org/en/countries/profiles/SLE [Accessed 17 Oct. 2018].
11. Ibid.
12. Harber, C. (2002). *Education, Democracy and Poverty Reduction in Africa*. Comparative Education. vol. 38 no. 3, p. 269.
13. Riddell, B. (2005) *Sierra Leone: Urban-Elite Bias, Atrocity and Debt*. *Review of African Political Economy*. vol. 32 no. 103, p. 126.

Chapter 3
1. Powell, L. (2010). *Beyond Beliefs*. [online] the Guardian. Available at: https:// www.theguardian.com/journalismcompetition/sierra-leone-street-children [Accessed 2 Feb. 2018].
2. *Mineral Resources, Their Use and Their Impact on the Conflict and the Country*. (2007). [ebook] Mineral Resources. Available at: http://www.sierraleonetrc.org/downloads/Volume3bChapter1.pdf [Accessed 17 Aug. 2019].
3. https://www.bbc.com/news/world-africa-13729504
4. Keith, K. (2012). *Blood Diamonds and War Crimes: The Case Against Charles Taylor*. [online] http://classic.austlii.edu.au/au/journals/SCULawRw/. Available at: http:// classic.austlii.edu.au/au/journals/SCULawRw/2012/7.pdf
5. Hope, Christopher. *WikiLeaks: Charles Taylor May Have $400 Million out of Reach*. The Telegraph. February 11, 2011. https://www.telegraph.co.uk/news/wikileaks-files/8319158/WikiLeaks-Charles-Taylor-may-have-400-million-out-of-reach.html.

Chapter 4
1. Beah, Ishmael. 2007. *A Long Way Gone: Memoirs of a Boy Soldier.* New York: Farrar, Straus and Giroux.
2. Edward Interview. https://www.youtube.com/watch?v=JcOplqsgTqQ
3. Serry Kargbo interview
4. Sesay, A. (2008). *Former Child Soldier Describes the Atrocities Committed by the RUF and the AFRC.* [online] International Justice Monitor. Available at: https://www.ijmonitor.org/ 2008/05/former-child-soldier-describes-the-atrocities-committed-by-the-ruf-and-the-afrc/ [Accessed 9 Apr. 2018].

Chapter 5
1. Ellis, Stephen. *The Mask of Anarchy: The Destruction of Liberia and the Religious Dimension of an African Civil War.* New York: New York University Press, 2007.
2. *V. Human Rights Abuses Committed By ECOMOG, Sierra Leonean Defense Forces, and Police.* Human Rights Watch. https://www.hrw.org/reports/1999/sierra/ SIERLE99-04.htm.

Chapter 6
1. Woods, L. and Reese, Timothy. (2008). *Military Interventions in Sierra Leone: Lessons from a Failed State.* Fort Leavenworth, KS: US Army Combined Arms Center, Combat Studies Institute Press, p.27.
2. Hirsch, J. (2001). *Sierra Leone: Diamonds and the Struggle for Democracy.* Boulder (Colo.): Lynne Rienner publ., p.54.

Chapter 7
1. Moiba, J. (2016). *Religion and Peacemaking in Sierra Leone.* https://pdfs. semanticscholar.org/ 3419/b76d114b83a4eb371bcd861cfe93c5f1ada6.pdf. pp.15-16.
2. Conteh, P. (2009). *Traditionalists, Muslims and Christians in Africa.* Amherst, N.Y.: Cambria Press, Appendix A.

Chapter 9
1. Mapendere, J. (n.d.). *Track One and a Half Diplomacy and the Complementarity of Tracks.* Culture of Peace Online Journal. [online] 2(1), p.2. Available at: https:// peacemaker.un.org/sites/peacemaker.un.org/files/TrackOneandaHalfDiplomacy_ Mapendere.pdf
2. Pham, P. (2004). *Lazarus Rising: Civil Society and Sierra Leone's Return from the Grave. The International Journal of Not-for-Profit Law,* 7(1), p.1.
3. The Truth and Reconciliation Commission Act 2000, Parliament of Sierra Leone, 2000. Accessed at: https://web.archive.org/web/20051230045239/ http://www.sierra-leone.org/trcact2000.html

Where There is Darkness, We Bring the Light of Christ!

Two-thirds of the world's population—more than 4.4 billion people—live in the 10/40 Window. Eighty five percent of those living in the 10/40 window are the poorest of the world's poor. Half of the world's least evangelized cities are in this window.

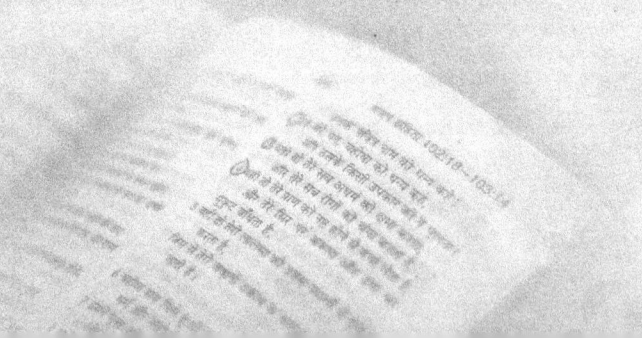

www.ingramcontent.com/pod-product-compliance
Lightning Source LLC
Chambersburg PA
CBHW032039040426
42449CB00007B/954